I'm very proud of this book, and you should be too. Just look at what people are saying...

"The only way this book could be any better is if K-von were 100% Persian."
  – *Maz Jobrani*

"I wish it was longer."
  – *Ex Girlfriend*

"English learn just to book read this!"
  – *Foreigner*

"Once in a generation a book comes along that changes the world. This isn't it."
  – *Political Commentator*

"Fun to read and tastes great, too!"
  – *Crazy Person*

"Written at a highly intelligent level and graciously dumbed down in the final edit, just for you!"
  – *Scientist*

"I think we should see other people."
  – *High School Sweetheart*

"This offended me to the point where nothing hurts anymore. I'm cured!"
  – *Social Justice Pioneer*

"He should have gone to law school."
  – *Parents*

"The perfect cultural text for anyone who is not Middle Eastern but has heard of that region."
  – *University Professor from Really Big School*

"Moo."
  – *Cow*

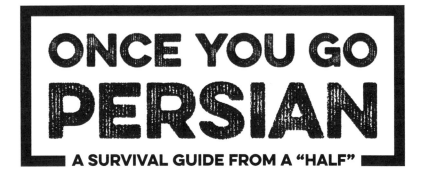

ONCE YOU GO PERSIAN

A SURVIVAL GUIDE FROM A "HALF"

K-VON MOEZZI

Cover photos by Mandee Johnson Photography | @mandeephoto
Cover and book design by Monica Chew and K-von Moezzi

TANX GOD! PRODUCTIONS
WWW.K-VONCOMEDY.COM

CONTENTS

PREFACE

CHAPTER 1: ½ PERSIAN 1
Cultural Thermostat | Iran Or Persia? | Growing Up In Reno

CHAPTER 2: A WHOLE NEW WORLD
(OF PROBLEMS) 13
Bedtime Stories | Iron Sheik | Check A Box

CHAPTER 3: THE COSTCO WATCHLIST 31
*Tanx God! | Persian Cucumbers | My First Mercedes
Comedy On-The-Side*

CHAPTER 4: NAKON 47
The Bad Words | Animal!

CHAPTER 5: LANDING A HOLLYWOOD
AUDITION 57
*Persian Restaurants | Paying The Bill | To Eat Or Not To Eat
This Is Good For That*

CHAPTER 6: DISASTER DATES 79
Persian Princess Codes Of Conduct

CHAPTER 7: MORE BLADES! 87
Laser Hair Removal | My Persian Nose

CHAPTER 8: LAW SCHOOL DEFERMENT 97
*Marvelous Maz | Dubai, Don't Buy | 3 Lonely Days In Dubai
Gaz-Plosion | Packing Heat*

CHAPTER 9: THE GODS MUST BE CRAZY 119
Bi-Polar Persians

CHAPTER 10: PERSIAN PARTIES 125
*The Art of Coming & Going | Persian Weddings | Just Married!
Meeting Family | Nowruz | Dancing*

CHAPTER 11: TANX GOD PRODUCTIONS 147
*TEDx Talk | Bed & Breakfast | Merchandise | What's In A Name?
A Persian Poem | Laugh 'Til You Cry*

CLOSING

SPECIAL TANX:

Angie Engelbert

David Shulman

Ellie Shoja

Millie Liu

Maryam Ekthiar

Monica Chew

Nikkisa Abdollahi

Mahta, Greg, and Eamon

Pam White

Pegah Sabeti

Toby Ogden

The Sweeneys

The McVickers

The Moezzis

...and too many more to list

Dedicated to Mom and Dad...

½ PERSIAN, ½ SCOTTISH, 100% FUNNY

PREFACE

At times I feel too Persian to fit in with Americans.
Other times, too American to fit in with Persians.
(It's time to realize, perhaps I just don't fit in!)

If you've ever felt this way, the good news is, you aren't
alone.

Multiracial kids often find themselves caught between
two worlds, yet still on the perimeter of both.

For many, this may feel alienating. Luckily, for me,
it translated into a career in standup...

This book will hit home to all the "halfies" out there... as
well as children of immigrants, and also to anyone who
was ever a child... yea... so, basically everyone will just
love this book. And that my friends is a NO MONEY
BACK GUARANTEE!

ALRIGHT, so we better get started. Some of these stories
will make you laugh, others will be touching... so if you
don't think it's funny; it's touching!

(...and if you don't find it touching, you're likely just
emotionally unavailable right now.)

Recalling these memories has been a treat and I thank
you in advance for reading this and allowing me to relive
them as well.

Consider this a survival guide on Middle Eastern culture
from an outsider who recently discovered all this himself.

Let's begin...

CHAPTER 1:
½ PERSIAN

It's official; I'm the most famous half-Persian comedian in the world! Coincidentally, I'm the ONLY ONE, so that definitely helps *(but let's not get hung up on semantics here)*.

My father was born in Iran, immigrating to the United States in his twenties. My mother, born in Iowa, eventually made her way to Nevada, where the two would eventually meet.

To summarize: Dad from the *Middle East* and Mom from the *Midwest*, raising a family in the *Wild-West*...

(Let's take a moment to compliment my father for being able to lock down an American woman in the midst of the Iranian hostage crisis. That takes skills!)

This unique mix allows me to joke about a range of topics that most wouldn't dare. License to be funny on some of the more sensitive issues in our world. A "free pass," if you will. *(At least that's what I must convince social justice warriors each night or else I'm out of a job!)*

Having a good sense of humor is essential in life, otherwise what's the point?! While some kids I knew were hiding Playboys from their parents, I was sneaking peeks at MAD magazine *(without my strict mother's permission)* thinking,

> "What better job could there be than making people laugh *for a living?*"

I then stumbled upon seasoned standup veterans like Robin Williams, Billy Crystal, Joan Rivers, and George Carlin. After that came the next generation with Chris Rock, Jerry Seinfeld, George Lopez and many more. These were my heroes; I just had to find a way to get from my living room into that TV with them.

Comedians fascinated me. With the right material they could change the way you thought about a subject, bring a household together with laughter, and make you feel like a member of their family too. I knew one day I wanted to connect people with laughter and build that same bridge.

What I didn't realize was, they take a lot of abuse in the process. The tolls you pay as a comedian come in several forms: online criticism, live hecklers, travel delays, bad auditions, rejection, and being apart from your closest family and friends. Sometimes, it's just a few of those. Others, it's all those and more. Perhaps that's why comedians are often represented with the face of a happy clown and a sad one. Also, those that stick with it understand that a tragedy today can often transform into your best material tomorrow.

One problem is, when done well, comedy looks too easy. I once had a really great comedy performance at a fancy event. The crowd laughed, applauded, and all was good. Then a violinist took the stage for a mere five minutes and received a standing ovation. Don't get me wrong, she was very good, but this wasn't exactly Niccolò Paganini we're talking about. I think people gave her much more credit because she was *holding a violin*! That was the difference. The audience can visibly tell how hard a violin is to play. Plus, there is a barrier to entry. Before you can *play* a violin you must *OWN* a violin. The audience knows they don't own one; they definitely can't play one, so now the violinist is in a whole other league. Respected. A standup comedian on the other hand... That's just some idiot talking into a microphone. The audience thinks, "Well hell, after a few drinks I could do that!"

When I get that vibe from an audience member, I sometimes invite them on the stage to give it a try. It's always fun for me...not so much for them. That is the moment the skill involved becomes a little more apparent to the audience. It's like my theory that Olympic events should always have one beginner athlete go first, before you watch the experts, just to give the viewer a sense of perspective.

"BEFORE MICHAEL PHELPS TAKES THE POOL, HERE'S BOB FROM A LOCAL APARTMENT COMPLEX — REPRESENTING UNIT 32C!"

At any rate, I've decided from now on, I'm going to start hauling a cello on stage with me to get the proper respect I deserve.

Performing for Middle Eastern audiences adds an extra level of difficulty for a standup comedian. Ask the crowd, "Who's never been to a comedy show?" and half the hands go up. Now you have to figure out how to make jokes about a culture that's not accustomed to being poked fun at. How to entertain transplants from a region where standup comedy is not a career option. How to get a "ha-ha" out of people from countries where jokes can lead to prison sentences, or worse. *(By the way, someone should tell those regimes that "dying on stage" is a figure of speech and not supposed to be taken literally!)*

No need to be too dramatic. Most of the shows I do take place in the United States where the crowds have a general understanding of how comedy works. Filling a room full of laughter on a nightly basis is quite the thrill even with all the ups and downs. I'm happy to report, "Standup Comedian" still lives up to my childhood hype as one of the best job titles in the world.

CULTURAL THERMOSTAT

With light brown hair and blue eyes, I'm basically an "Undercover Persian." Since I'm only half, I have to decide when to turn it up and down. I've developed an "Ethnicity Dial" on my "Cultural Thermostat," which allows me to select the proper setting as I so choose. You'll find me turning it up or down depending on the situation I find myself in.

My fellow "halfies" out there know exactly what I'm talking about. For example, if you're only half-Greek, but attend a Big Fat Wedding, you'll be turning that dial up. Half-Redneck, but find yourself at a Rodeo? Yee haw, you'll have it turned up that day for sure.

See, it's fun to come up with examples. You try...

I'm half _____, but when I attend a _____, I've got it turned all the way up!

I once saw someone trying to cut in line right in front of a black lady. That's when she warned,

> "Oh hellll no. You 'bout to bring out allllll the black in me!"

Apparently she too was a fellow undercover *"halfie"* and was about to "Turn Up" as well.

This is not an exact science of course — more like a feeling. Us "halfies" know instinctually when to dial it up or down depending on the mood we're in.

Personally, when headed to a nightclub with friends, I prefer to turn the Persian all the way up...*FULL BLAST.* Why not have some fun? I unbutton my shirt more than usual into a nice deep V-neck, letting my chest hair feel the breeze of the outside world. Bathe myself with a few extra pumps of cologne. I even walk more Persian *(which means hips forward and a scowl of confidence on my face).* If a beautiful woman walks by, my accent thickens to "fresh-off-the-boat" status, allowing me to stand out from the other potential suitors that evening,

> "Vell hello. How var you? Did you know once you go Persian ders no other version?"

Okay, let's be honest, it doesn't necessarily get me the phone number, but *always* gets a good laugh.

Other times I turn the Persian *down*. For example, when I go to the *airport*... That's a great time to *turn it OFF*. I also wear American flag boxers to demonstrate my patriotism in case I'm "randomly-selected" for a full TSA strip-search. *(I'm happy to report, so far it's never come to that.)*

Of course, "blending in" this well has its consequences. Often I find myself in the company of one group talking disparagingly about the other. Unaware of my background, they don't think to pull any punches in my presence. After all, I'm just a culturally camouflaged fly on the wall.

Here's a real life example of that. One time on a plane, a passenger seated next to me noticed a woman wearing a hijab boarding. He nudged me jokingly,

> "Uh oh — Looks like we got us some Middle Eastern people on the plane."

My reply,

> "Oh, you have NOOOO idea! They are literally everywhere."

It goes both ways. I've also hung around at late night hookah spots, listening as an entire group of Middle Easterners bad-mouthed my beloved America.

> "Americans dey are all fat losers vith no culture...uhh, except for you K-von..."

They caught themselves right near the end.

The comments on both sides range from silly stereotypes to deeply troubling. I take mental notes, looking to weave them into my act in ways that resonate, with hopes of one day getting a laugh and change some minds for the better in the process. This has become my life's pursuit, and that is what I will share with you in this book.

I think this is a fairly good time to mention: Ladies if you've NEVER dated a Middle Eastern man, might I recommend you start with a "half" first?...See if you like it. Test the waters. Dip your toe before you dive all the way in, just an idea. (If interested, you can find me on Google.)

IRAN OR PERSIA?

Before we go any further, we need to break down some controversial terms I'll be using. *Iran? Persia?* What's the difference? Which one should be used?

With a culture that dates back several thousand years, arguments ensue and classifications become far more confusing than they need be.

In an attempt to simplify it all: if you say "Persian" or "Iranian" everyone *should* know exactly what you mean. Anyone who gives you a hard time is being overly nitpicky. And while whole college degrees can be dedicated to the differences, here is my *very brief* explanation.

(Just so you know, I will now weather a lifetime of critical Persian/Iranian hate mail and nitpicking for the following explanation, so you better appreciate this.)

Once upon a time, the Persian Empire ruled most of human civilization. They conquered, thrived, and brought innovations we still use to this day like:

- Pajamas
- The Windmill
- Secret Service
- Navy
- Birthday Cake
- Ice Cream
- Tambourines
- Brain Surgery *(which, I'm convinced was a nose job that went too far!)*
- *...and many more. Look them up yourself.*

After centuries of battle with various enemies, the empire was reduced to an area we know as modern day "Iran." Put it this way, we call it "Germany" but they call it "Deutschland." Similarly, the West called it "Persia" while *the inhabitants* referred to it as "Iran." Around the 1940's the name was officially recognized as "Iran" by the entire world and started changing on all the maps.

Oh, and you know how the people from the "Netherlands" are known as "Dutch?" In a similar fashion, the people from Iran are often referred to as "Persian." It always makes me laugh when people criticize the region for having two names. *(Especially when pointed out by an English person from Great Britain who lives in the U.K.!)*

Iran was once a melting pot of diverse peoples, religions, and backgrounds. After the revolution in 1979, international conflict, and a hostage crisis, many fled the new Islamic Republic. To avoid confusion as to where their loyalties lay and to better fit in with their new communities, Iranians in America further adopted the moniker of "Persian" as their preference.

Me...I don't really care which name you use, so go with whatever works for you. I'll know what you mean. See, that wasn't so hard, now was it? Now if you'll excuse me, I need to go check my inbox and delete the hundreds of angry messages that just came in.

*(*4 months later — Yikes. Okay, I'm finally back.)*

GROWING UP IN RENO

Perhaps the main reason I don't care whether you use "Persian" or "Iranian" is that I am neither. I was born in Reno, Nevada. You couldn't find a town further away from Iran if you tried. It is literally on the other side of the world. *(Get a globe and see for yourself!)*

Thinking Reno was a hotbed for Iranian immigration in the late 1900's? You would be wrong. There was Dad and two others in town. Millions of Persians ended up in San Francisco and Los Angeles but somehow my dad stumbled upon Reno.

In my head, the story goes like this — My father was on a plane from Tehran to San Francisco. It stopped in Reno to refuel. He got off the plane to go "jeesh" (pee), took too long, and the plane left without him, so he decided to stay and make the most out of his new surroundings. *The End.*

My father's first goal when he arrived was to "fit in."

He bought a pickup truck, cowboy hat, married a blonde woman, and if anyone asked, insisted he was Mexican! Talk about living the American dream.

Note: It helps that the Iranian flag is strikingly similar to Mexico's. When entering America, simply turn your Iranian flag 90 degrees and you, too, can fit right in.

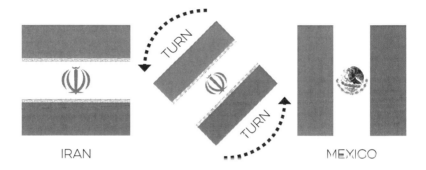

IRAN   MEXICO

My mom, brother, and I outnumbered Dad *(three Americans to one Iranian)*. Therefore, growing up, we did not learn his language or practice his religion. We did not drink his tea or smoke his hookah *(which would be odd for small children to do in the first place)*. We did not discuss backgammon strategy or Persian poetry.

Instead, my little brother and I attended all-American schools, played with our all-American friends, worked our way through the all-American Boy Scout ranks, while competing in all-American sports.

There was no Mercedes-Benz or BMW. No fancy Armani clothes, and no flashy gold chains around our necks. My dad didn't even own a bottle of cologne, and we definitely weren't rich. It's safe to say that as far as the stereotypes were concerned, we were the most non-Middle Eastern family you have ever known. Thus, people meeting us for the first time were extremely confused by our excessively ethnic names.

My brother, Shaheen, quickly changed it to "Sean." Brilliant! Somehow I missed that as an option. I was four years older and had been going by "Kayvaughn" for far too long. I stuck with it, even though "Kevin" would have made my life significantly easier.

Had I just made that simple adjustment, it would have spared me a lifetime of small talk. I am tired of detailing my family background, nationality, and heritage each time I simply give my name ordering a damn Starbucks! It's taken YEARS OFF MY LIFE, I tell you. *(That's why I wrote this book. Now I can quickly hand it to a barista and just get on with my day.)*

Then there are the skeptics who think I made my name up. What a treat it is, constantly hearing —

> "It's not REALLLYYY K-von, I bet. How'd you come up with that? Trying to be cool?"

Or...

> "Are just pretending to be Persian?"

Who the hell is "pretending to be Persian?" That doesn't happen.

Or my personal favorite,

> "So are you *trying* to be black?"

Yes, I'm *trying to be black*. Now if you'll excuse me, I'm late for my tanning session then off to get my corn rows put in.

CHAPTER 2:
A WHOLE NEW WORLD
(OF PROBLEMS)

School is always a *"real treat"* for those of us with ethnic names. *(Do you sense my sarcasm?)* With each new academic year, it takes the teacher about eight months to learn how to pronounce our names correctly. Of course, when they finally get it down, it's time to move up to the next grade and start all over again.

Oh, and if we have a substitute teacher — FORGET IT. For most students, a substitute means a day of watching movies and no homework. For us it means our name is about to be butchered during as the teacher takes attendance while the whole class laughs.

Roll call with a substitute teacher is quite possibly the most frightening thing I faced in my childhood. It would lead to a whole new slew of damaging nicknames and teasing from the other students for years to come.

My name is K-von Moezzi. Like "Mo"…then "ezzi" — it's NOT THATTTT HARD. Yet for some reason, it would always go something like this…

SUBSTITUTE:	CLASS:
"Robert…"	"Here"
"Jessica…"	"Here"
"Oh, this one… uh… …"	(me) "Here…"
"Hold on, let me try…"	"HERE! That's me I'm here!"
"Umm…ok, Kevin Mozello…"	*(whole class laughs)*
"Oh wait, Kalvin Martzi-nelli?"	"Dear Jesus…"

At this point, I'm crawling under my desk thinking, *seriously?*…That's not even CLOSE! Why are you *ADDING* letters!?! You know what, if you'll excuse me, I'm gonna go hang myself on the tetherball court now.

Bullies don't need any help from a substitute teacher to give you a hard time. Here's a tip; when introducing yourself to new people, quickly rattle off ALL the possible variations mocking your name *before* they can come up with them. Beat them to the punch. TAKE THE WIND OUT OF THEIR SAILS. For example, I always approach whoever looks to be the biggest jerk in the room and introduce myself.

> "Hi, I'm K-von. It rhymes with Avon. Or even Sav-On. Kinda like Caveman…"

See what I did there? Now he's got nothing left. A bully did once catch me by surprise, though. Not to be outdone, he walked away from my introduction and shot back,

> "I'll just call you GAY-VON."

Impressive. That was actually a new one. *Bravo, kind sir!*

I was spared from one fate that many "first-generation kids" face. Luckily my American mom was in charge of packing lunch. Therefore I had the standard issue "peanut butter and jelly sandwich in the brown paper sack"...*Just like everyone else.*

This means I didn't have to experience the horror of parents who insist on packing the "ethnic lunch" for their kids. We've all seen it before. Each day, children with immigrant parents shamefully wheel their family-sized coolers into school cafeterias across America. They reluctantly begin unpacking the plastic containers full of various items and sauces that require reheating in the teachers lounge. After that comes all the pouring and the stirring as the other students muffle their laughter. The lunch lady is over there trying to figure out if it's a meal or an unauthorized chemistry experiment. Now she's calling security, because, after all, "if you *see* something, *say* something."

To these parents — please, just make a sandwich and put it in a brown paper bag. All your kid wants to do is FIT IN. Leave the crock-pot at home. I implore you...

(I'm actively working on public service announcement to help put an end to this. I'm picturing a commercial with kids looking longingly into the camera, begging for standard lunch options, while Sarah McLachlan plays in the background.)

Big "thanks" to Mom for not putting me through all that. I'll take my string cheese and incredibly hard-to-pierce "Capri Sun" over ethnic school lunch any day of the week.

BEDTIME STORIES

As children, my younger brother and I were curious about everything under the sun. I now realize our parents had very different methods of dealing with our never-ending questions.

Mom would encourage us to conduct our own research, an academic approach that required effort on our part. So we stopped asking mom!

My Iranian father, on the other hand, relied on a method that can best be described as *"Make Sh*t Up."* He never admitted to not knowing an answer. Instead, unbeknownst to us, he'd invent one on the spot and make it sound somewhat credible.

This led us to believe that Dad was a wealth of information on just about any subject.

> Q: "Dad, why is the sky blue?"
>
> A: "Because God painted it blue with a giant brush."
>
> Q: "Why do boys and girls have different body parts?"
>
> A: "Girls used to have one, but if you put on a dress, 'it' falls off."

The horror! My brother and I vowed to never try on Mom's clothes; the risk was just too great. *(Bruce Jenner has proven Dad was both correct and well ahead of his time.)*

Similarly, when it was bedtime, Mom would give logical reasons as to why we should get our rest, yet we would defiantly refuse. That is when Dad would takeover:

"You don't have to go to sleep. Just close
your eyes so the sleep can't get in."

To me, *that* sounded like a much better idea.

Two things Persians are extremely good at are poetry
and storytelling. It must be in the DNA because my dad
was no different.

Most nights we were treated to a bedtime story. We were
always in the same configuration: my brother and I in
our bunk beds and my dad lying on the floor looking at
the ceiling, as he spun crafty tales in our darkened room.

Always a new story. Always fascinating. Always ending
too soon, leaving us wanting more.

This guy was like a real-life Scheherazade, the
storyteller from "One Thousand and One Nights." Look
her up. This was a clever woman who realized the king
was killing each wife after spending one evening with
her. *(An extreme version of what we call today, "hit it
and quit it." He would invite them over for "Netflix and
Kill.")* When finally called upon, Scheherazade cleverly
started telling the king a long thrilling story, refusing to
finish it just near the end. The king had no choice but to
spare her life until the next night. She would then finish
that story and launch into a new one, growing tired
once again before its completion. This lasted night-after-
night for well over a year; the king deciding he couldn't
kill this one, as she was far too intriguing. What a nice
guy! She saved her own neck by basically inventing the
"cliffhanger," which is a concept still employed by your
favorite movies, novellas, and reality TV shows!

I digress. So, our bedtime stories were a lot like that, but this was even better because he was our very own "Schehera-DAD!" His stories were bold, exciting, and full of plot twists. Some tales were scary and mysterious, while others were educational, teaching us the pitfalls of human ego and greed.

I had the coolest dad in the whole world. In comparison with my friends, while their parents may have *READ* them a story, my dad was the only one to actually *MAKE UP HIS OWN* each and every night, reciting it with no text to draw from.

Can you imagine the creative ingenuity? And, they were good stories too. One of my friends was skeptical. As I retold one of Dad's masterpieces about an ex-Green Beret who fought his way through the jungles of Vietnam armed only with a large hunting knife, my friend interrupted...

"That's Rambo."

Indeed it was! But how did this young man know my father's fierce tale of the great John Rambo?!

His reply,

"Because it's a movie, you idiot."

I was astonished. Had my father been secretly selling the rights to his stories and now they were being made into Hollywood blockbusters? We were always so poor; what was he doing with all the cash? *(Mom was not going to be happy about this.)* Eventually it sunk in; my dad was no Scheherazade, and these were not his stories after all. In fact, this was why he had such strict rules against us watching R-rated movies. It had nothing to do with the questionable content. His censorship was in place, so he could have a never-ending pool of source material to mesmerize his audience of two.

The jig was up, but as with the Tooth Fairy, Santa, and Easter Bunny, even as a kid, you know sometimes it's best to feign ignorance, keep your mouth shut, and stay on the receiving end of the gifts. That night, I let Dad tell us his newest story about an elite group of cocky Top Gun fighter pilots. We enjoyed it as always, without objection.

"Goodnight boys, and if you behave,
tomorrow I'll tell you the tale of RoboCop."

"Sounds good, Dad. Can't wait!"

Then with a smile, I rolled over and closed my eyes tight, *so the sleep couldn't get in.*

IRON SHEIK

"WWE" professional wrestling was a huge part of my childhood. Of course, at that time, it was known as the "WWF." Sadly for CEO Vince McMahon, the World Wildlife Foundation had also claimed those initials. So, one "WWF "was a collection of large wild animals that couldn't wait to mount each other, *while the other was a non-profit group for panda bears.*

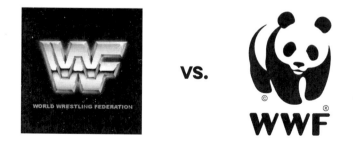

(Vince McMahon lost the lawsuit and changed it to WWE in the early 2000's)

As kids, we'd watch the wrestlers intently. When the program was over, we'd then practice those same dangerous moves on our friends. *(I'm not sure where our parents were at this time or why they allowed any of this.)* We took what we thought were appropriate precautions, always putting down a comforter or pillow on the hardwood floor before climbing a bookshelf and landing an elbow on our friend's neck. Safety first! Body slams, punches, kicks, slaps and death-defying stunts from the couch were all fair game.

Pro wrestling is basically a soap opera for men. The plots and characters mirror whatever real-world conflict is going on at the time and they provide a good/bad guy for that situation in the ring. For example, when we were involved in the Cold War, the biggest wrestling villain was a Russian guy. Each time Hulk Hogan beat the Russian, you felt like America had just won also. And fresh off the heels of the Iranian Hostage Crisis, nobody was more an enemy of the USA than Iran. Therefore, the Russian wrestler fell out of prominence and a new bad guy emerged, the infamous..."Iron Sheik."

Naturally, we loved to pretend to be our favorite wrestler while we watched. All the neighborhood kids wanted to be Hulk Hogan or the Ultimate Warrior. Sergeant Slaughter was a good one, too. So why is it that EVERY SINGLE TIME I'd go to pick a wrestling persona, my friends would interrupt —

"You have to be the Iron Sheik."

"AGAIN?! But I don't want to be Iron Sheik!"

"Too bad. You're the only Iranian we know.

Now throw this towel over your head and
go put on your pointy shoes."

"Ugh... fiiineee..."

Truth be told, the person portraying the Iron Sheik,
Hossein Khosrow Ali Vaziri, deeply loved the United
States. A collegiate wrestling champion, he moved to
Minnesota to help coach their university's program
as well as the U.S. Olympic Developmental team. But
every pro wrestling event needs a bad guy. A "heel." So,
the Iron Sheik dutifully stepped in, pretending to hate
America for the cameras.

My dad knew of this successful wrestler from back
home and was excited we now had a famous Iranian on
American television. Sheik would even say a few words
in Farsi before launching into one of his famous rants,

"Iran number von. USA, I spit on."

He became the guy America loved to hate. With every
appearance, it worsened global relations between
Iranians and the beer guzzling American demographic.
But it was just entertainment so my dad was proud of the
guy and had no problem showing his support.

While watching the program one evening a commercial
came on. The WWE was coming to Reno, right down the
street at the Lawlor Events Center. WHAT?! I hadddddd
to go. I immediately stopped choking my best friend,
released him from the "Camel Clutch" and slid into the
kitchen, already out of breath.

"Mom, DAD...Hulk Hogan. Wrestling.
They're coming...Here!!! We *have* to go!"

Mom wasn't into it. Dad shrugged with a maybe that didn't sound too promising. Why is it nobody seemed as excited as me about this? Then, a month later my parents surprised me with tickets to my first professional wrestling event. Dad said he would drive and my favorite uncle, Amoo Massoud also got roped into coming along. Oh, yea! The best gift a nine-year-old could ever ask for.

The day finally came. I put on my jean shorts, tank top, and tennis wristbands and headed to the car. *(You have to understand, this was high fashion for Reno at the time.)* I was almost out the door when my mother stopped me dead in my tracks,

"Where do you think you're going...?"

"WRESTLING! It's tonight."

"Not dressed like that you're not."

Mom always had a strict dress code when her kids left the house. She had this notion that we were always supposed to look "presentable." I was marched back to my room and forced to put on thick khaki pants, a long sleeve button-down shirt, and dress shoes. *(I was able to negotiate myself out of a tie.)* I'm not sure she understood this was a pro wrestling event *not a job interview.*

Catching my reflection in the mirror, I saw a young man that would one day make a fine accountant looking back at me. My dad whistled, it was time to go. Sulking my way to the car, my uncle was complimentary,

"You look good!"

Yea, *right.* I'll never get called into the ring to help Hacksaw Jim Duggan looking like this. As we made our way to the event Dad looked up into the rearview mirror,

"You see that bag on the floor? Open it up."

There in the bag was a YELLOW TANK TOP and my jean shorts. Oh wow! Just like what Hulk Hogan wore. I was back in business.

"Now, promise to put your dress clothes back on BEFORE we get home…"

"DEAL!"

We walked up the stairs into the cavernous stadium. I realized I was getting cold. *If only I had some thicker pants and perhaps a long sleeve shirt to keep warm…*but no matter, I'd soon be jumping up and down, pumping my fists, and warming up from the excitement that comes along with flying elbow drops and chairs to the backs of heads.

A sign was posted at the entrance:

"DUE TO A NECK INJURY, HULK HOGAN WON'T BE HERE TONIGHT. SORRY FOR THE INCONVENIENCE"

Noooooo! Now I'm dressed just like a wrestler who wouldn't even be there. The day had been a roller coaster of emotions. The usher informed us that Brutus "The Barber" Beefcake would instead be facing Bret "The Hitman" Hart. Well, I guess that was okay. I liked them too.

It was one exciting match after another. The music was booming. The cheap beer was flowing like wine…*and then came the Iron Sheik.* The whole stadium erupted into a "boo." I've never heard anything so unanimous — everyone, simultaneously showing hatred for the same villain at the same time.

All, except one man. One lone man, cheering for his fellow Iranian... *My father.*

What was he thinking? Even my uncle knew to lay-low in this situation. People started to take notice. I started to get nervous. It was only a matter of time before they put us on the "Jumbo Tron."

My Amoo Massoud and I did some quick math and agreed it was time to go. Hulk Hogan wasn't going to show up anyway due to his neck injury and there was a large chance we were going to leave with one as well. Maybe it was best to beat traffic and take off early.

Dad didn't want to go. We prodded him along as he attempted to get some final glimpses of the action. On the ride back I dutifully changed back into my Mormon Missionary outfit. Looking like a "jabroni" *(wrestling term for weakling)* I walked into the house excited to tell Mom about all the fun we had and explain to her the proper way to put someone into a "Figure Four Leg Lock." She patiently listened to all the intricate details and then I headed for bed.

Fifteen years later I would sit down with the legendary Iron Sheik for over an hour and share that exact story with him.

CHECK A BOX

Most people don't like being put in a box, but growing up, that's all I wanted. A box just for me. One to call my very own.

You see, whenever filling out any official paperwork at school in the 90's, there would be a portion where you were asked to claim your ethnicity.

1. Are you Hispanic/Latino?

○ Yes, Hispanic or Latino (including Spain) ○ No

2. Regardless of your answer to the prior question, please indicate how you identify yourself. (Check all that apply.)

○ American Indian or Alaska Native (including all Original Peoples of the Americas)

  Are you Enrolled? ○ Yes ○ No If yes, please enter Tribal Enrollment Number_____

○ Asian (including Indian subcontinent and Philippines)

○ Black or African American (including Africa and Caribbean)

○ Native Hawaiian or Other Pacific Islander (Original Peoples)

○ White (including Middle Eastern)

(sample of one of the many ethnicity forms we filled out)

You then had to scan the page to see which group best described your people. "Affirmative Action" programs in full swing, the further down the list you went the BETTER your chances of participating in government programs and attaining scholarship opportunities you desired.

The first time I saw one of these forms I didn't even know what it was for but I could hardly contain my excitement, "This is going to be good!" Soon I'd claim my rightful "victim status" in this fine country, changing my life for the better. Being of Middle Eastern descent would finally pay off. Apply my check mark in the appropriate area, and — PRESTO. The benefits would start rolling in!

Typically, the first category on the form was always "White." Ha! I'm sorry, but it's hard not to laugh. A pity knowing this box wasn't going to help anyone who "checked" it. Might as well start planning a funeral — this box was the first sign of death to all your dreams. There are no programs to help anyone who selects "White."

Next was "Asian." Yea, good luck with that. Seems like a decent minority, but there's too much competition there. These are all highly educated students with "Tiger Moms" — the kind that push their kids to attend learning centers for more school AFTER regular school. When that child finally gets home, there's a tutor waiting. After that it's time to practice piano, then help run the family restaurant. Thirty minutes before bed, the kid has to wake up and go back to school again. Asian kids go eighteen years with straight A's and no Zzz's.

The next two boxes were a toss-up: "African-American" and "Hispanic." Both strong selections. One could check these knowing good things were on the horizon. You may have never been to Africa but on "box-checking day," you were as "African" as can be. You could be a blonde-haired, blue-eyed kid with a great-great grandmother who lived so far north in Spain people swore she was French, but on box checking day YOU GOT TO BE "HISPANIC."

Then came the absolute best box, one that had no rival: "NATIVE AMERICAN." Oh man. Every student was tempted to scratch it with his or her #2 pencil just once to see what might come. We struggled with the consequences and formulated our alibi if we were to get caught...

> "Whattt... how in the world did *that* happen? Must have smudged it by mistake."

We meant no harm. We were young. Curious. Just wanted to know what it felt like. Of course, while tempted, none of us actually had the guts to do it, except for one kid, whom from what I understand is now a high-ranking Chief operating a casino in Idaho. *Good job, Thomas!*

Below that was: "Other." How boring is that? That box was just there for people who didn't want to select "White." A consolation prize to pacify the masses and keep protesters from rioting. As if to say,

> "You can be 'Other.' THERE. Are you happy? Now, go on, back to work!"

ALL of this was great and all, but where the hell was *MY* box? "Middle-Eastern?" Surely that region deserved a box; war, fighting, discrimination, hate crimes, religious disagreements, and injustice around every corner. How can I be expected to excel in this country with no box?!

I took one of these forms and marched right up to the teacher's desk to explain my predicament. I was making an attempt to justify my minority status, fully aware that my future hung in the balance,

"Ms. Fredrickson, I'm a little confused by this form. My father is Middle Eastern, which, if you look here on the map is close to Spain — so, 'Hispanic.' But technically it's on the continent of Asia. So, there's that...Let's not forget that Iran is near Egypt in Africa —

She cut me off,

"Check 'White.'"

"Yea, I can see how you might think that... but I don't believe that truly defines who I am inside."

"WHITE."

"That...is...definitely an option. Here's a thought. You see Ms. Fredrickson, I was wondering if I might be able to check ALLL the boxes since there seems to be some confusion —"

"GO SIT DOWN!"

"Yes, ma'am."

Defeated, I headed back to my desk, made sure she wasn't looking — then checked "OTHER."

TAKE THAT, MS. FREDRICKSON!

*Update: Now "Middle Eastern" is officially a box —
along with so many other boxes that they no longer mean
anything. In fact, the selection of boxes is now longer than
the test itself!*

Check all the boxes of which best describe you:

What Color Are You?

☐ White   ☐ Black   ☐ Beige

☐ Vhite   ☐ Brown   ☐ Roy-G-Biv

What Ethnicity Are You?

☐ Latino   ☐ Wu-Tang   ☐ Pacific Islander

☐ Hispanic   ☐ African   ☐ Native Islander

☐ Asian   ☐ Wakanda   ☐ Atlantic Islander

☐ Middle Eastern   ☐ Native   ☐ Highlander

What's Your Deal?

☐ Handicapable   ☐ Allergic   ☐ ADD

☐ Male   ☐ Sexual   ☐ ADHD

☐ Female   ☐ Asexual   ☐ HDMI

☐ Both   ☐ Bisexual   ☐ AT&T

☐ Gender Fluid   ☐ Trisexual   ☐ LGBTQ

☐ Undecided   ☐ Pansexual   ☐ RSUV

☐ Confused   ☐ Bowlsexual   ☐ WXY & Z

Now you know your ABC's next time won't you pee with me?
(continued on next page…)

CHAPTER 3:
THE COSTCO WATCHLIST

Everyone loves *buying* things from Costco. My father loves *returning* things there. A long time ago, they made a grave mistake by announcing their policy:

*We will take back *anything* at *any time*.

This may or may not be a Persian thing, but because of this policy, my father actually gets excited when something in our house breaks. He stands in the living room and proudly declares,

"It's ok. We go to Costco!"

The key word is "we" because this is now a *family* trip. We head to the store together, shuffle through the return line, exchange our items for store credit, and then go shopping for new ones.

And no matter how many times we successfully pull this off, it is always stressful and embarrassing.

While standing by his side, I've witnessed my dad return many things to Costco, testing the limits of his $65 yearly membership.

(*The price may have gone up by the time you read this so don't write me asking where you can get a discounted

membership. Please just keep reading.)

ITEM: **REASON:**

TOASTER   *there were too many crumbs at the bottom*

PRINTER   *it ran out of ink*

CLOTHES   *the color faded after 14 years of washing*

He even once got away with returning something he *didn't even buy* from Costco.

The absolute best was when he attempted to return our big old TV from the family room. *(You know, the ones surrounded with wood?)* When asked why he was dissatisfied, his answer,

> "It's too big, doesn't fit in the house, we want to exchange it for a flat screen."

The lady looked at the receipt, then back at him with disdain,

> "...For *nine years* it hasn't fit?"

(They made a rule shortly after that, putting a two-year limit on returning televisions, which I believe was in direct response to our family.)

The last time we went, the cashier looked up his account history and informed us that somehow he'd returned more items than he'd ever bought from Costco. They gave him a warning that this would be the last time they'd accept a "return" and that his account had now been "flagged" nationwide.

We walked those aisles that day for what I knew might

be the last time. You could feel a sense of loss and hopelessness in the air.

A week later, something in our house broke. We all looked at Dad trying to figure out how he would respond.

He sat for a long moment scratching his chin, then had an epiphany,

"It's ok. We go to *SAM'S CLUB!*"

TANX GOD!

Want to speak like a Persian? Follow these easy lessons:

First, we must work on counting:

1 = Von

2 = Two

3 = TEREEEE

Good! Now that you have that down, we're ready to go into sentence structure.

LESSON #1
First speak extra slowwww and rearrange the words and drag them out

What are you doing?	=	*Whattt you are doingggg???*

LESSON #2
Put "e" before every word that starts with "s"

If you are smart	=	*If you are esmart*
you still show up to school	=	*you estill show up to eschool*
seven days a week	=	*eseven days a week*

LESSON #3
Change all "w"s to "v"

What are you doing...	=	*Vhat you are doing...*
in a BMW that's not white?	=	*in a BMV that's not vhite?*
Just borrow mine, you're welcome	=	*Just borrow mine, you're velcome*

LESSON #4
Take all h's out of words that follow a "t"

Thank God	=	*Tanx God!*

That last one with the *h's* caused me a lot of problems. Most kids love to play video games. However, Middle Eastern parents are so serious about education that video games are expressly forbidden on school nights.

The lecture I received from my dad was,

> "Video games are for eSaturday, eSpring
> Break, eSummer Break, but definitely not
> for eschool niiiight."

So, the goal becomes to get your schoolwork done and "esneak" in the video games when you can.

My friends and I did just that one afternoon. Dad was at work, so the coast was clear. We quietly popped my newest game into the Nintendo console and pounded away on our two-button controllers. We were having a blast.

Yet, there's something strange about Iranian dads. I truly believe they are able to hear their children having fun no matter where they are in the "vorld." For no reason whatsoever, he returned home from work early that day, made his way to the bedroom, and kicked open the door to find four children breaking his rules. We sat there in horror, the looming shadow of an angry Iranian father cascading over us.

> "Vhy are you playing video games? You
> must estudy."

Then he launched into a passionate lecture about his own scholastic abilities...

> "In Iran, I estudied hard. I graduated tird
> IN MY CLASS."

My friend chuckled

> "You were... 'turd?'"

> "Yes, and it wasn't easy being tird. I had

to push and push and earn that tird all by
myself."

I objected in horror,

"DAD, you weren't *TURD*."

"I VAS TIRD! In Iran, the top estudents
get escolarship. First, esecond, and then
me...tird. Tanx God for that!"

And with that, he unplugged our Nintendo and walked
out of the room with it...

*(At this point, some of you still don't know what is so
funny about the word "tird." There is a double meaning
there. Take a timeout and ask an American to define the
word for you, then come back to reading.)*

Another way my father would instill the value of
education upon us was to declare,

"K-von, you must get good grades. If you
don't, you end up working at McDonald."

*(*Middle Eastern people never pronounce McDonald's
with the "s" at the end. It is always singular: McDonald)*

Ironically, each time my brother and I received good
grades, as a reward, my father would take us to
"McDonald!"

Kind of a mixed message if you ask me! I guess in his
mind, bad students *work* at "*McDonald,*" while good
students *(and their fathers)* eat there.

PERSIAN CUCUMBERS

Fitness, athletics, and outdoor activities were always mandatory growing up. The electronics craze was just getting started, and my dad wasn't going to be an early adopter of the Atari or Nintendo. *(After all, they didn't sell those at Costco yet.)*

For the first twelve years of my life, we had no video games in the house and whenever I was bored, my parents had one answer:

"Go play outside."

Those born after 1990 may find this to be a foreign concept:

"What exactly would you play outside?"

Well, you would just make up a game. Hitting dandelions with a stick...that was a game. Terrorizing anthills was a game. Trying to stomp on your little brother's shadow whilst he tried to step on yours was a very serious game *(that always ended in tears)*. I realize these are not the most advanced activities, but it was what we had at the time.

When we were finally old enough to participate in organized sports, my parents pushed me into swimming.

On the plus side, swimming is a low impact, full-body activity that wears you out. The downside; it is the most anti-social sport in the world. Your head is completely underwater. Communicating with others is impossible. Meanwhile, you absorb toxic chlorine chemicals directly into your brain. All of this explains my current lack of social skills, and so much more.

They also put me in cross-country running *(the second most anti-social sport in the world and hardly fun for spectators).*

> "Hey, I'm heading off into the woods, be
> back in 30 minutes. Root for me!"

(Looking back, I'm realizing my family may have been trying to go as long as possible without hearing from me.)

What my parents didn't account for was, swimming two miles a day paired with running all over the world increased my endurance to uncontainable heights. Their goal was to wear me out, yet now I had plenty of energy and stamina! The unforeseen outcome; they'd created a monster.

The biggest problem with swimming competitively is the speedo. In the last ten years, the industry has done some amazing things with Lycra technology, making these bathing suits look more like shorts, boxers, even pants. Something a superhero would wear. But in the 80's, there was but one option, and you know which one that was. The "European cut," "show off everything to the world," tiny "bikini underwear" swimsuit that everyone cringes when they see.

Of course, with an Iranian dad, this was already his swimsuit of choice, so I was unaware of its unfortunate social status. Only in *hindsight (bad choice of words)* is this painfully obvious, as we flip through the family photo album.

On my first day of swim practice, my dad also told me some fun facts about swimming in his home country.

> "In Iran, we put cucumbers in our swimsuit. When you swim in the ocean and get salt in your eyes, you pull out the cucumber, break it in half, and rub your eyes. It removes the salt naturally...then you *eat the cucumber!*"

What the heck was he talking about? This must have been before the advent of goggles. But I find it hard to believe that a "cucumber in the speedo" was ever the best solution for "salt in the eyes."

There are questions that go along with a story like this:

- *How do you keep a cucumber secure in your suit while swimming?*
- *Where do you put the cucumber — front or the back?*
- *How many cucumbers would you go through for an average day at the beach?*
- *Do you have to wait 30 minutes to swim after eating said cucumber?*

Most alarming of all is that Persian cucumbers, while delicious, are very small. Who wants to emerge from the ocean with a tiny one bouncing around in their swimsuit?

(I vowed to find a standard American cucumber if I were to ever go the traditional route and give this a try.)

After months of swim practice it came time for my first swim meet. The pressure was on. I was nervous. My mom told me the rules and what to expect:

> "No matter what, keep swimming until you finish."

"What if my goggles come off?"

"YOU KEEP SWIMMING."

Got it. There I was, seven years old, standing high on the diving blocks above the pool. Over the speaker we heard,

"25-yards Freestyle. Take your marks!"

— BEEP!

We all dove in — and *THAT* is when I remembered I was supposed to tie my speedo. To my horror, the force of the water brought that swimsuit down around my knees!

Now, what?! As you'll recall, Mom said to keep swimming, so I did. With each stroke, I desperately tried to grab my suit and yank it back up, but to no avail. I needed to end this race fast and fix this.

In the final few yards, kicking was getting harder as my suit had now become "ankle cuffs." To my credit, I did not stop. Touching the wall first, I'd won the race!

Instead of cheering my victory, there was laughing and pointing. I got out of there in a hurry. *(No comment on whether or not a cucumber was lost in the process.)*

MY FIRST MERCEDES

There comes a time in every Persian's life when they get their first Mercedes. For some, it doesn't happen until later, but it eventually happens. For me, it was when I turned 16 on the dot. Like I said, we weren't *that Persian* and we didn't have *that much money.* So the Mercedes we acquired was not what you might expect.

The day I received my driver's license my dad threw open the door to my room, his voice booming with pride.

> "K-von, you're 16 now. You are my #1 son. Therefore, in the garage for you is a new MERCEDES"

And with that, his eyes sparkled.

> "What? No way?!"

> "Go. Check it out!"

I ran to the garage...*and then my heart sank.*

There it was...the most run down, beat up, sorry excuse for a Mercedes you have ever seen in your life. The hood ornament was dangling downward toward the radiator. The color was a brownish paint combined with rust and primer *(so we'll just go with "off-silver").*

I recognized this car immediately. It had belonged to a distant relative who decided to get rid of it because it had over 200,000 miles. *Naturally, my father wanted "in" on that action.*

This thing came fully loaded with cracked leather seats, stained carpeting, wood floors, broken speakers, and springs that squeaked long after going over a speed bump.

Best of all "NO AIR CONDITIONING" because who needs that during 114+ degree summers in Las Vegas? They say, "It's a dry heat." Well, tell that to my *(insert body part here)!*

My 1st Mercedes

Sensing my displeasure, my dad had a response for every objection...

"What's wrong? It's Mercedes!"

"...You said it was new."

"It's new to us!"

"Dad, it's a DIESEL!"

"... but it's TURBO!"

"This car is five years older than me..."

"Which makes it a CLASSIC!"

You don't want to look a gift horse in the mouth, *(especially when you know it likely has advanced dental problems)*, instead I reluctantly got behind the wheel and decided to make the best of it. Before I could put the key in, Dad stopped me, giving detailed instructions on how to properly start the car.

- *Turn the key halfway.*

- *Allow the engine coils to warm up for three minutes.*

- *A light will go on alerting you the engine is ready.*

- *THEN, turn the key and fully start it.*

- *Let the engine warm up for 5 minutes before driving.*

By the time I completed the process I'd missed a week of school. When I finally pulled out of the driveway that afternoon, diesel engine roaring, squeaking down the street on worn out shocks, many philosophical questions ran through my mind:

- *Much like, if a tree falls in the woods does it make a sound; is having a large back seat a good feature if no girl wants to get in it?*

- *Shall I enroll in auto shop class to ensure this hunk of metal keeps running?*

And, most importantly —

- *What are the odds that I'll be able to return this thing to Costco?*

COMEDY ON-THE-SIDE

Anyone with immigrant parents knows they provide an endless supply of material for a potential comedy act. Those same parents however, would never consider a career in comedy to be a viable option.

In the Middle Eastern community, there are standard careers that we all feel pressured into. These are professional occupations with a heavy emphasis on education; doctor, lawyer, and engineer are the big three.

Real Estate and Architecture were just approved this year by the Council. Congrats!

Of course, entrepreneurship is also permissible. As we hinted toward earlier, you can *own* a McDonald's; you just can't work at one!

Coincidentally, the same week I decided to pursue standup comedy full-time, my brother found out he was accepted into USC, one of the top dental schools in the nation. My parents were the most proud *and* the most disappointed they had ever been at the same time.

This affected my dad more than I realized. One day he burst into the house announcing he had a plan for me.

"I did some thinking. You can be a doctor."

"No Dad, we already went through this, I want to be a comedian."

"Son, you can do both!"

"Dad, you have to focus on just one. Comedy is not all fun and games. It takes all your heart!"

"You aren't using your brain. I figured it out. You can be a Urologist."

"Huh…"

"Urology…Go look it up."

Like most twenty-year-old men, I had no clue what a urologist was. I searched online as my dad peered over my shoulder, reading aloud —

Urologist: *A doctor who specializes in urinary issues.*

Dad nodded in approval.

"Dad, why would I become a *'urologist'* when I want to be a *comedian?*"

"Because the two go hand-in-hand. You make people laugh. They pee their pants. You hand them your card and say, 'Come see me in the morning.' Then you fix that problem, too. *MORE BUSINESS FOR YOU!*"

CHAPTER 4: NAKON

Catch me performing at a Persian event, and by the end of the night, without fail, I'll be cornered by a handful of ladies telling me I should learn Farsi. *(If you see this happening, please come save me.)*

The conversation always goes like this...

> "Vhy you don't speaking that vhich is Farsi?"

Was that even English? I politely try to explain that no one else in Nevada really spoke the language so it simply wasn't on my radar, growing up.

> "...but vhyyyyyyy???"

I try to let them down easy, clarifying that I'm basically an all-American kid with merely a dad from that part of the world.

> "...but vhy your dad did not teach you???"

I calmly say, he was at work all day and quality time with family was limited, so we didn't use it for linguistics.

> "Eh, such a shame. Very disappointing to hear. You really need to learn. Your family

did a very bad job with this."

As you can see it builds from polite conversation into inquisition and crescendos with full-blown "language shaming." I feel the need to defend myself but don't want to lose my patience. I have to carefully consider which of the following defenses to employ...

Defense #1: The Counter Attack

Um, excuse me, but I live in America...where we speak SPANISH, lady!

Defense #2: The Poor Me Plea

I can't even go to Iran. The strict religious government jails artists, makes comedians disappear, and doesn't allow for freedom of speech.

Defense #3: Going Global

There are over a billion Indians and that country is next door to Iran. How come you never learned Hindi?

Defense #4. The Abstract Assessment

I will learn the language when they can agree on what to call it!

The community is at odds with whether it is "Farsi," "Persian," "Parsi," or something else. The only thing they *can* agree on is: DON'T YOU DARE CALL IT <u>ARABIC</u>! *(That's the same as meeting someone from Korea and saying, "Oh, don't you guys speak Japanese?")*

By the way, I'm not kidding when I tell you I'm encouraged to learn Farsi at every opportunity. One nice grandmother told me,

"You must date the Persian voman. If you dating Persian voman, you vill learn Farsi!"

She was so sure of it; I decided to give it a try. I dated a Persian woman for two years. I only learned one word: *Nakon* (pronounced "na-cone").

Nakon, when used on a date, is a way for the girl to shyly say, "no" or "don't," but it in a way that *almost* sounds like, "Maybe next time." *(And trust me, it's <u>always</u>, "Maybe next time.")*

Whether it's to hold hands in public, put an arm around her during a movie, or go in for a kiss after the date... any attempt at flirting and you will likely become an expert in the many uses of *nakon* as well.

Admittedly, one very good reason to learn Farsi is so when you're standing in line and hear two Iranians gossiping, you'll know EXACTLY what they are saying about you. Even if you don't speak the language, trust me, *they are talking about you.* Simply hiss *"Nakon"* at them and storm out. This will leave them embarrassed, thinking you understood their every word.

I never picked up on the language because the only time my dad would speak Farsi to me was when he was yelling at me. That's why, for the first 5 years of my life, I thought my name was "Pedar Sag!"

That's one of the most common swear words you'll hear. It means "your father is a dog." The funniest part is the one that always calls you that is *YOUR FATHER*. He's literally referring to himself. *(Whether he realizes it or not is up for debate.)*

My dad made an attempt to educate us on his native tongue, but while he could *speak* it, he definitely wasn't good at *teaching* it. Suffice it to say, his method was hardly that of the good people from "Rosetta Stone." To help us along, he decided to name our pets with Farsi names. *As if anyone could possibly learn an entire language this way.* There aren't enough animals on Noah's Ark to learn a whole language, but that did not deter him.

We had a dog. He named it "Sag."

Sag means dog.

So I had a dog, named "Dog." That sounds like something straight out of a Johnny Cash song.

He brought home a blue bird and named it "Aubee."

Aubee already means blue.

By the age of thirteen, all I could say was "sag" and "aubee." I'm in the house yelling "blue" at the bird and "dog" at the dog. Any Iranian friends that came to visit must have thought I was in "special ed."

It is true; I was developmentally challenged in the language department, and Dad was to blame.

Congratulations. You now know just about as much Farsi as I do. Now, let's learn some more together.

One reason I find the language difficult to grasp is that it has its quirks. For instance, if you say "gol," it means "flower." And as we know, "aubee" means "blue." But if you say, "gol-aubee," that means "YELLOW PEAR." *WTF?!*

The dialect is very flowery and seductive. If you want to say, "I love you," you might say, "jigar bokroham," which translates to, "I want to eat your liver."

What kind of love is that?!

Want to say, "You are so cute?" "Moosh bokhoratet," which translates to, "a mouse should eat you."

As you can see with Persians, almost everything revolves in some way around eating.

Probably the most confusing of all are the "bad words," which are without a doubt, a favorite of Iranians. Again, Persians have poetry in our soul, in our language, and yes, that bleeds over into our "swear words" as well. Once translated, a Persian insult can be so beautiful it brings a tear to your eye.

*Side Bonus: Become familiar with the bad words and you'll be able to hold a basic/functional Farsi conversation!

THE BAD WORDS

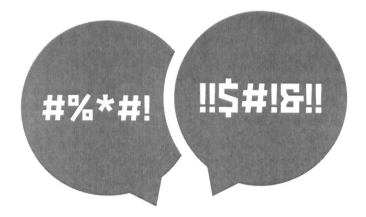

"Khak Bar Saret"

Translation: *May we put dirt upon your head.*
Intended Meaning: *You are so ignorant that you should die and we toss a shovel full of dirt on you just to do you and your family a favor.*
(Remember, this is very rude).
English: YOU'RE STUPID

"Heyfe Noon"

Translation: *You are not even worth giving bread to.*
Intended Meaning: *You are clearly a useless creature occupying the planet for no purpose and deserve no food.*
English: YOU'RE A WORTHLESS IDIOT

"Zahre Mahr"

Translation: *The poison of a snake.*
Intended Meaning: *May you take enough poison from a snake that it permanently silences you.*
English: YOU NEED TO SHUT UP

"Bi Sar-O-Pa"

Translation: *You are without head or feet*
Intended Meaning: *You are an uncultured "low-life" who must crawl on the very ground that the rest of us walk on.*
English: YOU'RE A WORM

"Goh eh Sag"

Translation: *You are no better than the excrement of a dog in any way.*
English: *self-explanatory

"Toke Meh Sag"

Translation: *To me, you represent the balls of a dog and all that goes along with it.*
English: YOU'RE A SON OF A B#@*H

As you can see the poor dog takes a lot of flak. What did the dog ever do?

...and last but not least:

"Hayvon"

English: YOU'RE AN ANIMAL

ANIMAL!

Not sure why I'm expected to know Farsi when my uncle, Amoo Abas, has lived in America for 40 years...and every year, his English *gets worse!*

It's unbelievable! We as a family aren't even sure how it's possible. He used to talk to us and made an effort to communicate in English, but Abas is an efficient man. He discovered long ago he could get through most of his days in the United States by reducing his vocabulary to one word: *Animal.*

Each night Amoo Abas (Uncle Abas) sits in front of the television and just shouts, "Animal!" when he sees something he does not like. It's an umbrella statement that can be used for almost anyone...

Kanye West,

"Animal!"

The Kardashian Family,

"Animal, animal, animal, animal!!"

Caitlyn Jenner,

"Two type of ANIMAL!!!"

The best part, all politicians immediately fall into the "animal" category — across the board. That is one thing I love about Amoo Abas, he is bi-partisan, fair, and balanced. We could all learn a lot from this man. He serves as a beacon of hope. A reminder to us all, that these so-called "World Leaders" are the ones that deserve our ire, not our loved ones closest to us. And he does this by vocally showing his distaste to all politicians from the comfort of his recliner. With each appearance on TV, they've voluntarily put themselves on his chopping block.

George Bush appears,

"Animal!!!!"

The leader of any Middle Eastern country,

"Animal!!!!!"

Barack Obama,

"ANIMAL!!!!!!"

...and the one good thing I can say about President Donald Trump winning the election, he's single-handedly *tripled* my uncle's English. Each time Trump appears on TV we hear,

"BIGGEST ANIMAL EVER!!!!!!!"

When you think about it, Republicans, Democrats, donkeys, elephants, at the end of the day they really are just...ANIMALS!

CHAPTER 5:
LANDING A HOLLYWOOD AUDITION

Early on in my comedy career, I was called in to audition for a new television show embarrassingly called "HOT GUYS WHO COOK."

 If you haven't seen it yet, online search: "K-von Cooks Persian Food," then come back to this.

Millions of people all over the world saw this appearance, but few know the story of how I landed it *(or what it takes to land any audition in Hollywood for that matter).*

The audition process is daunting. Casting directors are trying to pick one or two individuals for a TV show and will often go through two thousand people to find them. When you finally land a role, it was as unlikely as getting into Harvard! *(That should give Middle Eastern parents a new respect for what we do.)*

Near the end of the process, they whittle it down to the last eighty guys or so. You've come so far and yet still nowhere near the finish line.

Since this show was called "Hot Guys Who Cook" and would appear on the "Food Network" they asked us to come in and explain what dish we would make if given the chance to be a chef on the show. I showed up unprepared. Unsure what I would cook but hoping that it would magically come to me.

For almost two hours, I sat in that waiting room as guys went in one by one. I nonchalantly put my ear against the wall and could actually make out what they were saying in there. The conversations became routine,

> "If we select you for our show what would you make for us?"

I heard each of the responses,

> "...Spaghetti"

> "...Pizza"

> "...Lasagna"

"...Spaghetti with a side of lasagna...and a slice of pizza."

There was exasperation in the casting director's voice... *then it hit me.* This woman was bored. I needed to TURN THE PERSIAN UP. After all, there's no better cuisine in the world than Persian food. Why didn't I think of this before?! It had slipped my mind, but now I had my angle.

It's the end of the day now, and they finally call me in. Upon first glance, they saw just another typical American guy. Their expectations were low. The casting director dutifully pushed record on the camera and repeated what she'd already said no less than one hundred times before,

"If we select you for our show, what would you make for us?"

I tilted my hips slightly forward.

I undid a button on my polo shirt to expose the appropriate amount of V-neck.

I thickened my accent ever so slightly to emphasize the names of the dishes,

"For you, because you are so beautiful, I would make the most delicious zereshhhhkk polo. Along with jooojehhh kabob."

She damn near fell out of her chair.

"I'm sorry, I wasn't expecting that. Can you please repeat that again for the camera?"

"No problem, but first let me remove one
more button. Ahh, that's better. As I was
saying, for you, I would make zereshkkk
polo with jooo-jehhh kabob."

After that, she stopped me.

"Hang tight, the Executive Producer is
right next door. I think she may want to
hear this."

She returned now with another lady, clearly her superior.

"Please tell Julie one last time what you'd
cook?"

At this point, I'm running out of buttons. I unfasten one
more. It's all or nothing now. I have my *Persian Dial*
turned up to uncharted levels, and worried it just might
break...

"Vell since now der is two of you, I
would make for you zereshkkkkkkkk
poloooooooooo, and joojehhhhh kabob and if
you are lucky, masto khiarrrr."

Their cheeks became flush. They hadn't been talked to
like this all day *(and perhaps never in their entire lives)*.

The producer mustered up what was left of her breath
and asked,

"And what exactly is zeresh kabob and polo
abdul and that other stuff you just said?"

I turned the Persian back down. No need to hurt anyone.

"It's a really delicious rice with citrus

chicken and refreshing yogurt on the side.
You'll like it."

As I buttoned my shirt back up, collected my belongings
and headed for the door, they held a little pow-wow.
Before I could turn the handle, they blurted out,

"Congratulations. You're on the show.
We film in three days."

I acted cool, told them I couldn't wait, and thanked them
for the opportunity...but inside I was jumping for joy.
Soon I'd be on national television cooking a very delicious
dish.

On the car ride home, I called my Ameh (Aunt) Shirin to
tell her the good news.

"Ameh, you aren't going to believe this.
I'm going to be on TV!"

"Good Boy!"

"We film in three days!"

"Okay, we will be vatching and tape it!"

"Yes, it's a show where I'll be cooking
zereshk polo and joojeh kabob."

There was silence, then

"...But. Pedar sag, you don't know how to
cook zereshk polo and joojeh kabob. Vhy
did you tell them you can do that?"

She was right. I did not know how to cook zereshk polo *or*
joojeh kabob. That is why I had called her. I knew I was

in good hands since no one cooks better than my Aunt Shirin. As long as she walked me through her recipes, I'd be fine in time for the taping. I mean, how hard could it be?

My friends — it was at this moment I learned a valuable lesson. Middle Eastern women know how to cook the most amazing food in the world, but THEY HAVE NO CLUE HOW TO *EXPLAIN IT.*

They've been doing it too long. There are too many little nuances. *(And between us, I secretly think they don't want anyone to be able to replicate their culinary skills.)*

This became apparent when over the phone the directions became exceedingly difficult to follow.

"First get a pot..."

"Okay, what size?"

"Umm, a good size pot..."

"Okay, now what?"

"Now put rice in the pot..."

"How much rice?"

"Just pour the rice and look at it. You vill know."

"Ummm, okay."

"Now put vater in the pot..."

"How much water, Ameh?"

"Up to your FINGER."

My finger? These are not exact measurements we're talking about here. And we haven't even got to the joojeh kabob.

Thoughts of hopelessness began running through my mind.

"What have I done? I am going to be a failure on national television!"

And,

"My father was right, I should have become a UROLOGIST!"

During my trial runs, I became increasingly worried since I was never able to get the rice quite right. Sadly, the time to film was upon us. I'd soon be portrayed as an expert Persian chef and would fail as the whole world watched.

The crew put up large lamps to properly showcase what was about to go down as I set out all the pots and pans. Soon cameras were rolling. I went through each of the steps I'd been taught over the phone, but I clearly lacked the same confidence I had during the audition.

I tried to distract the audience by juggling tomatoes and talking about the healing power of lemons. However, the moment of truth had come. It was time to show off the traditional rice that I was supposedly an expert in cooking. I flipped the pot over, tapped the bottom with a wooden spoon and offered a prayer to the gods. Looking into the camera I muttered,

"I now present to you 'zereshk polo'…"

You could hear a pin drop. My Ameh Shirin must have been there in spirit throughout the process. I lifted the pot from the plate that afternoon, and for the first time in my life; I looked down to see the most perfect rice I've ever cooked!

This masterpiece stood there like a lavish rice castle. In fact, the golden "tadeeg" was there on top, right where it should be. Every fan of Persian food knows "tadeeg" — the pan-fried crispy rice that forms on the bottom of the pot that we playfully fight over. The Spanish refer to it as "socarrat," Koreans "nurungji," and Dominicans "con con," but we all know it universally as "very tasty."

As a chef, "tadeeg" is your gold medal for a job well done. This also gives you an idea as to how amazing Persian food is. Even the burnt stuff is delicious.

You may be questioning why you've had Persian food but this is the first time you're hearing about "tadeeg."

It's because WE DON'T SHARE IT WITH YOU. Iranians are generous with almost everything, but not that. "Tadeeg" is made available only by demand.

PERSIAN RESTAURANTS

When Americans are craving something a bit more exotic they may consider Indian, Mexican, Thai, or maybe sushi. What a shame Persian food doesn't register higher on that list for most. It is delicious, palatable, and easy on American taste buds. While you can easily whip up taco night from home, so much effort goes into Persian food you're better off going out, letting someone else do all the hard work for you.

"But K-von, we don't have any Persian restaurants in my town."

You may want to check again. Some communities have a restaurant owned by an Iranian that has been cleverly labeled "Mediterranean" on the sign. That's to trick racist people into stopping by. *(The owner can also easily claim to be Greek if another hostage crisis were to go down.)*

Large cities will have an easy-to-find authentic Persian Restaurant. The menu will not have Greek gyros or falafel from our Arab friends. Don't worry; you won't end up eating camel or horse. And no matter how nice the restaurant, most are still oddly attached to a general store where you can buy recipe books, candy, spices, and CD's of Persian singers you've never heard of on your way out the door. *(I'm still trying to figure out how to get my DVD in there, if you have any contacts.)* Now let's take you inside so you know what to expect.

SEATING...

When you sit down at the restaurant it won't be on cushions on the floor. You will be in a regular chair. Only two Persian restaurants I've ever been to had a belly dancer so you shouldn't count on that either. *(If a number of dancers keep approaching you for money, you most likely went to the wrong address. That's a strip club, you idiot. GET OUT OF THERE!)*

A plate of radishes and leafy greens will be placed on the table along with flatbread, butter, and onion. Most Iranians can eat an onion like an apple if you let them. *(Just do not let them tell you any secrets after that.)*

You'll want to try a little of everything your first time, so go with more than one person since the portions are "family-style."

Oh, and before we get into the dishes, there will be yogurt. This will be a reoccurring theme for the night. Mexicans have salsa, Asians have soy sauce, and Persians have our yogurt. Yogurt on everything! Think I'm kidding? They will even put yogurt in carbonated water, shake it up, and hand it to you as a beverage to go along with your yogurt-topped food. *After all who doesn't want a nice refreshing yogurt soda (doogh) on a hot sunny afternoon?*

APPETIZERS...

In my opinion, we are a little lacking in the appetizer department. Most of the offerings are in the form of dip for the delicious warm flat bread. Perhaps deliberately boring to keep you excited for the main course. Here are some of them...

KASHKE BAADENJAAN: Eggplant Onion Garlic dip
Do not eat if you have a date you plan on kissing anytime that month.

MAAST-O-KHIAR: Yogurt with cucumber, onions, mint, and pepper

DOLMEH: Grape leaves stuffed with rice

MAIN COURSE...

Here's where Persian food truly shines. You won't be able to get enough of these items. There are far too many, and too many variations of each to list, so here are a few of my favorites.

All are full of spices but none are "SPICY"

THE RICE DISHES...

ZERESHK POLO: Delicate saffron rice with delicious little tart berries in it.

ALBALOO POLO: The sweeter variation to Zereshk Polo with juicy dried cherries cooked and blended into the rice.

SABZE POLO: Rice with herbs and greens cooked into it. Get your salad and your rice at the same time!

LUBIA POLO: Green been and tomato rice. Sometimes with small pieces of beef in it. A whole meal in itself.

TADEEG: Delicious, crispy rice from the bottom of the pot. *(Remember: They may lie and say they ran out. Tell them you will wait and do not accept "no" for an answer.)*

THE MEAT DISHES...

JOOJEH KABOB: Delicious spiced citrus chicken cooked on a skewer
Pay attention to your plate. Someone will try to steal a bite.

BAARG KABOB: Tender filet mignon cooked on a skewer
You can use the skewer to fight off your family members.

CHICKEN KOOBIDEH: A long strip of flavorful ground chicken cooked on a skewer
You'll thank me for this one.

BEEF KOOBIDEH: Ground seasoned beef on a skewer
Puts any hamburger patty to shame.

SOLTANI: A meal that includes two meats above
Order this one. It's the combo plate!

(If this appears black and white, get a crayon and color it yourself. Full color printing costs $6 extra per book, so I decided to save money like a true Persian.)

THE STEWS (a.k.a. Khoresht)...

All the stews go on top of the rice.

GHORMEH SABZI: A stew with dried lemon, kidney beans, and various greens
When done right, this takes several hours to make and often has beef or lamb in it. Hard to describe and impossible to forget.

GHEIMEH: Meat, tomato, and split pea stew which sometimes comes with thin french fries on top as a bonus!

FESENJOON: Walnut and pomegranate stew

DESSERT...

Once again, we're a little lacking when it comes to dessert. I call it "desert" because most of the cookies are so dry and powdery you'll be begging for water. Those that aren't, are drenched in honey and sugar, far too sweet to consume without getting a cavity. *(Although, many Persians are dentists, so this may be how they keep their businesses profitable.)*

The following are my favorite dessert items...

GAZ: Nougat that's thick, taffy-like, with pistachios embedded in it.

PERSIAN ICE CREAM: Persians arguable invented ice cream and if not, they sure perfected it. They add pistachios and rose water or saffron to it, which gives it a unique taste. Much better than boring old vanilla.

FRUIT: Nature's dessert. My personal favorite. Persians *"get it right"* by offering a large supply of fresh fruit after every meal. Eat plenty of cherries, watermelon, and grapes. That's all you really need anyway.

OTHER THINGS YOU MAY WANT TO AVOID:

KALIPACHE: Sheep head, brains, and hoof
...Need I say more? That sounds really BAA-AAD!

TEA...

CHAI (rhymes with "Try Me"): An unspoken rule is: After dinner, you must have tea. If you are in a Persian home and refuse, they will bring it to you anyway. It will arrive at a temperature of no less than 2,000 degrees Celsius. The tea will not cool for several hours forcing you to sit in the living room and discuss politics well into the night. If they bring you tea, also ask for a bucket of ice to go along with it so you and your family can leave before sunrise without burning your throat.

— OKAY, and with that, let's all go take a food break!

PAYING THE BILL

At the end of the night, the owner of the restaurant will probably come out to greet your family and ask what you thought of the food. It is customary for the owner to offer your meal for FREE...DO NOT ACCEPT IT! The custom is it is now your turn to argue with this person for the chance to pay for the meal.

I get it. It will be hard. American chain restaurants have undermined this long-standing tradition. At Applebee's, if the manager says you get a free meal you say,

"Hell yea!"

But in Iranian culture, this offer is just a way of being polite. The owner will say something like,

"I cannot accept your money here, you are my guest."

Then you are supposed to say,

"No, I insist."

At some point, the owner will put on an act and begrudgingly take your credit card *(while inside breathing a great sigh of relief)*. Your card will then be quickly swiped before anybody has a change of heart.

*Don't be surprised if you are not offered your food for free. This tradition is going away because too many Americans do not know the delicate dance that we just discussed and it puts many Persians out of business.

That "dance" is called "Taarof" *(also spelled "Tarof" which rhymes with tar-loaf)*. I call it extreme kindness and overboard hospitality. Iranians are raised to taarof and what was meant to be a nice thing, at times, becomes a real problem.

This generosity is often on display in various forms. In a taxi, the driver may tell you, "I can't charge you for this ride." Or at a party if you compliment someone on a piece of clothing they may try to give it to you.

This happened to me once. At an event I noticed a gentleman wearing the most hideous coat I've ever seen. I regrettably started up a conversation with some small talk,

"Hey, nice jacket."

He perked up,

"Please my friend, take it, it's yours."

Oh, no! Now I'm involved in a taarof war. It happened THAT fast. I declined,

"No, no, please I like it, but on you!"

"No, you like it and therefore, you must have it."

To my chagrin, he forced it into my arms and had me try it on. Now, I'm wearing the ugly jacket at the party. Several times I went to remove it but he was always watching me. Waving at me. Giving me a "thumbs-up" from across the room. The coast was never clear.

It wasn't until I got back to my place that night — I looked left, then right, made sure he hadn't followed me home, and at last, threw that damn thing away.

Two months later, I saw the same guy at another event. He came right over to me and asked how much I liked the jacket. I was embarrassed but also only half-Persian, therefore, not bound to the unwritten law of taarof. I didn't keep this charade going any longer and was completely honest with him,

"You know, I never actually liked your jacket. I was just trying to be nice. I threw it away..."

There, I said it. I braced myself for a long lecture on how rude I was and how no "true Persian" would ever do such a thing. I was not ready for what came next. The man leaned in, with his "fresh-off-the-boat" accent,

> "I tell you secret. I saw guy vearing that same jacket and told him I like. He forced me take it. Vhen you said you like, I couldn't vait to get rid of it and give to you!"

Not only was he NOT MAD, but our overly polite Persian culture had kept this jacket in rotation long past its due date. If it weren't for me, that hideous thing may still be circulating through our community to this very day.

Now, back to *paying the bill*. That is a bit of a misnomer because when two Middle Eastern people eat, they don't pay for the bill, they *FIGHT OVER THE BILL*. You just got done arguing with the owner about paying, but that was merely the warm-up. The true test is fighting over the bill with friends and family, and it is an integral part of the evening. I'm sure when it started it was all in good fun, but over the past several thousand years, it *(like most things from the region)*, has become more extreme.

Here is the proper way to fight with your guest over the bill:

First, you put your hand on the bill and explain why you must pay.

The other person will then try to take it from your hand and say,

> "No. Please, you are my guest."

Now you must increase the level of drama,

"It would be disrespectful for you to pay."

Then they will take it too far,

"You don't understand, if you pay you will
have offended me and several generations
of my ancestors, I MUST PAY."

If it ends there, you got off easy. There are tactics you
can utilize to where the bill will never come. Many know
the whole, "I'm going to the bathroom" trick where you
secretly slip the waiter your card. To my family, these
moves are for mere amateurs.

My father and his brother (my Uncle Massoud) have
fought over the bill for 60 years. They've become experts.
One time my uncle went to "use the bathroom" and was
shocked to find that my father HAD PAID WHEN HE
WALKED IN. That's right, prior to ordering or anything!

The next time we went to eat, my uncle sat there
laughing. My dad asked what was so funny. The bill
never came. My uncle revealed he'd CALLED IN HIS
CREDIT CARD NUMBER OVER THE PHONE.

The last time we ate my uncle grabbed the bill without
a fight from my father. He put his card in the booklet,
handed it to the waitress, declaring,

"I WIN!"

Moments later the waitress came back and told him his
credit card wasn't working. My uncle looked at my dad
and right away knew something was up.

Dad leaned in,

"I CANCELLED YOUR CARD!"

This was some next level stuff. I don't think my uncle Amoo Masoud will ever be able to beat that, but I'm sure he spends many nights tossing and turning trying to devise a plan.

Therefore we simply must end this chapter with TO BE CONTINUED...

One Last Note: No matter who pays, both parties complain about the other on the car ride home.

TO EAT OR NOT TO EAT...THAT IS THE QUESTION

Ameh Shirin may have taught me how to cook over the phone but it's far better to sit back as she does her thing in the kitchen.

Iranian women can be some of the most gracious hosts in the world, and that is on full display around mealtime. They won't let you lift a finger. Your only job is to relax and marvel as the plates of food arrive.

And don't think you are just going to have a small sample of anything. Oh no. My aunt wants you to eat -eat -eat. After five helpings she then offers you more. If you finally refuse, her face falls,

> "Oh...I see...you didn't like my food... Maybe I cooked the chicken too long..."

> "WAIT, WHAT?! NO, it's just I was full four plates ago!"

She will look at you, defeated, as tears begin to form in her eyes. You'll then agree to have just one more helping.

Then she'll be happy again. That's just the way it goes.

There is a bit of a double standard here as well. While they encourage the men to eat unnatural amounts, they may simultaneously pull a female family member aside to scold them,

> "Akshhh...no more or you'll never find husband."

I think this is part of a much bigger conspiracy where Persian women always want to look better than the men.

Female willpower is amazing. At one event, I was seated next to an elegant Middle Eastern lady. Soon, some of the best dessert you've ever tasted arrived. She had one bite, agreed it was delicious and pushed her plate aside. With a mouthful, I asked,

> "This is so good, are you sure you don't want anymore?"

Her reply was poetic,

> "You know, the last bite tastes exactly like the first but contains *allllll* the calories."

Wow. That was pretty deep. That was a good one! I made a mental note never to forget those wise words *and then reached for her plate and polished that one off too.*

What can I say, I'm a bit of an ANIMAL!!!

THIS IS GOOD FOR THAT

The older women in the family not only gladly serve you the food but also will provide you with a medical reason as to *why* you need to eat it. There is no scientific basis to any of this. It's simply ancient wisdom passed down for generations and accepted as fact. Some things seem more realistic than others.

> "You must eat spinach; the iron in it is good for your muscles."

> "Please have Sumac; it helps remove the cholesterol from the beef."

> "Baba, onion is very great for your heart."

> "Have some lemon; this will improve your circulation."

The food item and what body part it supports constantly changes from one meal to the next. One week, pomegranate is good for your liver; the next it improves hair growth.

I'm working on a handy tool so anyone can easily provide the same sage advice. On one side, spin the dial of various food items. Then spin the other for a body part, and *bingo* — There's your answer! (*Patent Pending*)

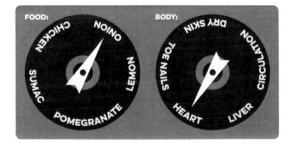

CHAPTER 6: DISASTER DATES

Now it's time to get into the intricate and difficult mind of the "Persian Princess." Many of you will read this and say, "This does not apply to me!" GREAT. But be honest, you know *somebody* like this. Maybe she's a friend, sister, or co-worker. Before you share this book with her, tear these pages out so as not to offend.

If you are reading this and the pages below are missing, you know what that means...

 CUT HERE

ASKING A PERSIAN PRINCESS TO...

...TAKE A PHOTO

A Persian Princess will always stop the rest of the group from taking a photo until she is ready. First she must get into position, turn to her favorite angle, check her makeup, put one hand on her hip, toss her hair to one side, pout her lips, and only then is the group allowed to proceed with the picture. *(She then will have to approve of it, and most likely announce to the group that they must do a retake.)*

...CALL YOU BACK

A Persian Princess is married to her phone. She looks at it 24/7. Nevertheless, when you ask why she didn't call you back or respond to a text, she'll claim she didn't see it. She may even claim her phone died over the weekend. In reality, a Persian Princess would rather die herself than let that happen to her beloved phone. If you hint that perhaps she is lying *you are very rude.* You will never know the reason *she* didn't respond, just know that it is *your* fault in the end.

...DRIVE SAFELY

A Persian Princess is not capable of driving safely. How could she? She is far too busy entertaining her friends in the car, conducting a video call with her mother, checking her eyelashes to make sure the adhesive is holding, and pretending not to notice other drivers vying for her attention, all while operating a new foreign car she isn't comfortable driving yet.

...WORK

One of the hardest things to do is get a young, rich, spoiled, Persian Princess to work.

A few years ago, I was hired to perform comedy in a wealthy family's living room. Before you laugh, this was one of the most opulent mansions I've ever been inside. The attendees were all VIP's (Very Important Persians) who preferred to have the entertainment come to them.

Prior to the gig, I told three other comedians plus two magicians to clear their calendar and join me for the event. After hearing the pay, they jumped at the opportunity.

With a week to go, the clients made one last request:

> "Please bring a bilingual and pretty
> Persian girl to bartend for two hours."

I was told the thirty people in attendance would likely order drinks that were very simple to make, and the pay would be $1,000.

I'm thinking,

> "Sure, no problem. How hard could that be?"

I immediately texted a Persian girl I knew to let her know I had a decent paying job waiting for her, but after two days, there was no reply. *(Her phone must have died.)*

I moved on to another friend and told her we would be working together with excellent pay and would love to have her there if she could make it. She claimed to already have plans that night and quickly got off the phone. I don't even think I'd told her which night it was yet.

A handful of other ladies also came up with various excuses why they couldn't be there. I was shocked. How was I failing to fulfill the client's request?

With only one day to go, I was getting desperate. I called one last friend, asking her what she was doing Friday night. She said she was available.

GREAT! I explained how bad I needed her help and provided the details. I'd be doing comedy and she'd pour drinks from behind the bar. Then we visit, eat delicious food, and in under two hours we'd be done for the night. There would still be time for her to go out with friends afterwards if she wanted.

I blurted out,

"Oh and the best part, it pays $1,000!"

There was a long pause. Then she slowly said in a much thicker Persian accent than I'd heard from her,

"You...vant me...to be bartender...?"

"...Yea! I mean, well not like a 'bartender,' but just for the night, I need someone to join me. It'll be fun! Thirty people..."

She started "turning up" the Persian,

"I just vant to make sure I'm hearing you correctly. Let me get this straight, you... vanting me...be bartender."

Her English was getting worse,

"...umm, I mean. Two hours...$1,000..."

She was appalled,

"This is your American side coming out. I am Persian girl. I can't believe you asking me to bartend."

"Well, I...wait, what?"

She went on to deliver a long lecture berating me for asking her to do such a thing. She told me her father raised her better than that and demanded to know how this would look in the community if anyone were to find out?

Based on the reaction, you would've thought I asked her to be a topless pole dancer for the remainder of her life. I defended myself,

"This is ridiculous. It's a lot of money, and you're simply handing them beer or wine. Mayyyybe pouring a 'vodka-cran' at the most. This is not hard. Plus consider it networking with the right people."

She shrieked,

"I am not BARTENDER!"

I yelled back,

"LISTEN, I'M NOT A COWBOY BUT I RODE A HORSE LAST SUMMER!"

That's when I heard her slam the phone down on the other end. *(Which, she then had to pick up and push "End Call.")*

Needless to say, she did not bartend that night. I had to let the booking party know that I'd failed to cover that final request for the evening. They ended up hiring a Mexican woman who did a fine job, got a huge tip, and she now works for them regularly, putting her 5 children through college on the generous income.

It is safe to say I learned a lesson that day. It is also safe to say, I'm still not quite sure what that lesson is. I guess it's: **Don't you dare offer a good paying job in a nice environment to a Persian Princess and think you are just going to get away with it, buddy.**

We're still looking for a pretty Persian bartender. If you know anyone who needs a quick $1,000 tell her, I apologize in advance for disrespecting her, and to email me.

...GO ON A DATE

Did you know the Middle Eastern word for "dating" is "MARRIAGE?" Going on a date is just not something that was done in the past. *You either want it or you don't — No test drives!*

Luckily, times have changed and restrictions are loosening up a bit. Some of our readers have enjoyed this book so much they are now seriously considering dating someone Middle Eastern. You may even be thinking, indeed, it would be best to start with a "half" first, and to that I applaud you. This section is for you.

THE MEN...

People think Persian men are too controlling...it's not true. Look, as long as the girl I'm dating checks in with me, tells me where she's going, when she'll be home, lets me go through her phone, and does exactly as I say, I let her do whatever she wants...*(*For the most part.)*

THE WOMEN...

Oh, you think the men are bad? If dating is hard, then *dating a Middle Eastern girl is the Olympic level.* Just to give you an idea, there is a Saudi man who divorced his bride recently just two hours after their million-dollar wedding. The reason? Once they arrived at their honeymoon suite, she wouldn't get off her phone and pay a little attention to him. Don't believe me? Look it up. The world heard this and was shocked. I was not.

Here I will outline some of the major differences one can expect when dating a Middle Eastern woman:

If you ask a woman on a date, she may meet you there. *A Middle Eastern woman expects you to come get her.*

A girl over twenty-one will often live on her own or with roommates. *A Middle Eastern girl lives with her entire family until you marry her. Then she moves them in with you; now you have roommates.*

A date with most women involves a night alone to get to know her better. *A Middle Eastern girl brings three cousins and a best friend along. (This has happened to me more than once.)*

On most dates, the girl may reach momentarily, as if to pay, and then let you refuse her offer. *A Middle Eastern girl will reach to push the bill closer to you (and remind you to also pay for her three cousins).*

At the end of the night, walk most women to the door and you just might get a kiss. *A Middle Eastern woman runs into the house, slams the door, locks it, puts the chain in the door, sets the alarm, wakes her parents up, calls the police, reports someone loitering in her driveway, turns on the floodlights, and over a loudspeaker warns you that in 10 seconds she'll be unleashing her dog. 9, 8, 7...*

I've walked my date to the door once only to have her go inside as her mom gave me a guilt trip,

> "Oh, finally she is home. I was so vorried she was out so late."

"Late? It's 11pm."

"Yes, but she's so young."

"Your daughter is 32!"

"Yes, but very innocent for 32..."

The mother then thanked me profusely for returning the daughter safely and proceeded to offer me fruit for the road. I was stunned. There, neatly wrapped in paper towel, was a washed pear, nectarine, and two plums.

On the way home, my friend called and asked about my date.

"How did it go? Did you get any?"

My response,

"I got a nectarine! From what I understand, that's pretty good."

I guess the fruit was some sort of consolation prize. It turned out to be very good for my digestion *AND* my rejection, but somebody still owes me that kiss.

CHAPTER 7: MORE BLADES!

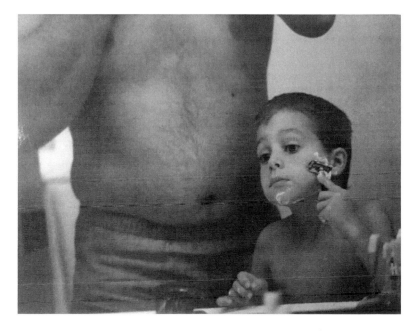

Earliest known photograph of K-von shaving, although he started several years before this.

Having dark, luscious, exotic, voluminous hair has its downsides. It often makes its appearance all over our body. The typical Persian "five-o'clock shadow" comes in before noon. It's the only time something Middle Eastern arrives early to anything.

Because of that, we do it all...wax, shave, bleach, and pluck for hours...*and that's just this little area between our eyebrows.*

This is no quick thing. We set aside some time weekly just for hair removal maintenance. I call that period "Tuesday."

The razor blade companies have recently done their best to tackle the problems we face. I'd like to take a moment to highlight the honorable Gillette for leading the way. For the longest time, men had just one blade on their razors. I am talking several hundred years. Then came the "Sensor Excel." This had two blades AND an "Aloe Cooling Strip." A nice start, but they knew that was not going to be enough.

Next came the "Mach 3." Three blades to handle the problem. Persians could now shave three times faster than before. What would we do with all the extra time? Spend it with our family? Travel? Learn a foreign language? The options were endless.

Three blades could have held us for a while but the blades kept coming faster and more furious than ever before. The "Fusion 5" delighted with an unprecedented FIVE BLADES! And this time, it vibrated. *(Who asked for that?)*

All these advancements in shaving led me to secretly believe perhaps a Middle Eastern executive had worked their way to the top of the organization. Was a *Habib* now handling hair removal? Was a *Raj* now running the razor department? Was a *Behzad* begging for more blades? Was a *Cyrus* calling for more cutting edge... *(okay, this had gone on far too long).*

We may never know. All I can tell you is that my hypothesis will be proven correct if Gillette ever unveils the shimmering, shiny, "MACH VON-HUNDRED." Fully equipped with 100 rows of glistening blades, one simply drags it up one side of their body and down the other, then – *boom!* Hop in the car and head to work!

(I just hope they don't forget the "Aloe-Cooling Strip" on that one. We're definitely going to need it.)

LASER HAIR REMOVAL

Middle Eastern people spend plenty of cash on various hair removal tactics, but there comes a time where we all must seriously consider the nuclear option..."LASER HAIR REMOVAL."

As a half-Persian, I only have half as much hair. My heart goes out to all the "fulls." The question is where do you go and whom do you trust when making this leap?

(Persians may want to consider buying the whole laser as a long-term cost-saving measure. Plus, brings the family together!)

When you aren't looking, you don't realize ads for businesses that offer laser hair removal are *everywhere.* Then, once you're in the market, you can't help but notice the myriad of choices. Doctor's offices, skin clinics, and fly-by-night operations advertising on billboards, bus stops, and local publications all over town.

In some facilities, lasering hair is all they do. Others offer it as an additional service at a tanning salon or even in a dental office. What an odd pairing. How does that go down?

"The dentist will be right in to see you.
Please open your mouth and take off your
pants so he can get started right away."

Must be for people who are *very* busy. I can't help but
picture hair flying everywhere while the patient's mouth
is secured wide open with a dental dam. NO THANKS.
We're going to have to keep those two visits separate!

I researched a bunch of companies online, found the one
with the best reviews, and headed in for my consultation.
I imagine this situation to be far more comfortable for
ladies, as it's more socially acceptable for a woman to
seek out innovative ways to improve her looks. A man
discussing his hopes and dreams for his body with
a stranger is just shameful *(unless you are in West
Hollywood)*.

The clinician sat across from me with a hollow outline of
a genderless human and asked,

"Which area would you like to focus on?"

I grabbed her pen and circled the whole picture. I
mean if we're going to do this, let's go all the way. In
fact, let's make it fun, like pin the tail on a donkey. I'll
stand against the wall. You crank up the laser, put on
a blindfold and start zapping whatever you come into
contact with. May the force be with you!

She explained that is not how it works and that we
needed to focus on regions.

I discovered something else that day. The further down
you go on these "regions," the quieter and more timid

your voice gets. Mine started off with great confidence,

"MY NECK, WE MUST DO AROUND MY NECK. And SHOULDERS."

Then my voice diminished ever so slightly.

"Of course, armpits would be nice."

Now, at a much lower volume...

"And...belly."

I leaned in, voice trailing off into a whisper...

"...and thighs...maybe you could do my upper...thighs...while you're down there."

"No problem," she flatly said. "Nothing to be worried about. We do those areas all the time."

Relief.

She scratched the estimate on paper and slid it over for my approval — $500.

"Hey for all that? A little pricey, but not bad."

"Per session.

"Oh..."

"With a mandatory six sessions."

"YIKES. $3,000?"

"Yes, but you're buying all those Fusion blades. I've done the math for you and as you can see here, this will practically pay for itself after just...40 years."

"I see."

"And the good news is, as our ad here states, 'We guarantee no more hair after just six easy sessions.'"

"Ah! Well, that sounds nice."

You only live once; it might as well be hairless. *Let's do it!* We shook on it, and she ran my credit card.

Little did I know I was signing my own torture manifesto. It was *supposed* to be pain-free. It was *supposed* to be easy. But what came next zapped me to my core. *Literally.* Think of the laser as one of those neon bug lamps. And you know that horrible noise those things make each time a moth is electrocuted? That's the delightful SOUND I heard for each 45-minute session. Whenever the laser hit a patch of Persian hair it was the sound of "death to a thousand insects."

The stomach is especially bad. I put on my headphones and played music while praying to all of the various gods people believe in, just to get through it.

CIA: if you are reading this, *and we know you are*: Forget waterboarding! Simply "laser" the terrorists. They'll gladly reveal information about the innermost workings of their organizations just to make it stop. I'm hereby proposing we bring that laser to Guantanamo. *(Civil rights activists, YOU STAY OUT OF THIS or you're next.)*

Over the course of a year, I subjected myself to this time and time again. The worst part, after each visit, *the hair came back.* What happened to truth in advertising? Three months after the final session, I stormed back into her office to tell the lady I was not happy with the results. Sure, it was *LESS* hair but what about her "guarantee?"

Her reply,

> "Well, it looks really good. I am not sure why you're upset."

Not sure?

> "Because I still look like a teenage Chewbacca. You promised it would BE ALL GONE. REMEMBER? THE AD... The ad you showed me with the '*six easy treatments?*'"

I was sure that ad was long gone. The ole bait-and-switch. But as luck would have it, she pulled it out of her desk!

> "This one."

> "Yes! That's it."

She then redirected my attention to the little disclaimer at the very bottom. I couldn't believe it. How did I miss that before?

There in size 6-font with a tiny star, it read:

*Persians and Armenians <u>NOT INCLUDED</u>

Damn. I should have known. There's always a catch.

MY PERSIAN NOSE

Persian cucumbers are small, but our noses are not. Iran is the nose-job capital of the world. It is a sign of wealth to have your snout worked on and so common that it's hardly something to be ashamed of.

In America, no woman admits to having a nose surgery done for aesthetic reasons. They'll make up any excuse other than; they hated their nose.

> "You don't understand. This was a medical emergency. I *HAD* to do it."

Usually, they blame a "deviated septum."

Um, yea, their septum "deviated" from allowing them to be beautiful.

Or, they did it because they had a "breathing problem."

SUREEEE…You mean every time you looked in the mirror, you started hyperventilating.

In Iran, they don't play that game. They have their noses done with pride. I've heard that some women will leave their bandages on their schnozzle long after the required time to signal their improvement, while others may even wear bandages on their nose having never done the procedure in the first place!

None of this was relevant to me since I was born with my mother's American nose: straight, small, and pointy. The kind of nose that Iranians pay big bucks for. That is, until I went kayaking in Chile. Let me explain...

Kayaking is a sport where you strap yourself into a little tiny boat and pray not to drown. Beginners should start in a swimming pool. I started in Chile's famous Futaleufú River, one of the more difficult areas. My little brother and I were on a weeklong rafting expedition, and I decided kayaking couldn't be *THAT* hard. It was time to learn. I begged the guide to borrow his kayak, shrugged off some quick tips and headed to the river.

One skill everyone in a kayak needs to learn is "rolling." When you flip upside down, you need to quickly put your head towards the front of the kayak, pull hard with your paddle, and you will pop right out of the water — upright and breathing fresh air once again. At least that's how it's supposed to work *in theory*. Easier said than done.

That day in the river I found myself upside down. I needed to roll back up. I put my paddle in and pulled but not quite hard enough. Barely moved.

On the second try, I pulled even harder. I almost got up and around, but not quite. FAIL. Now I'm still underwater, running out of air, and now fifty yards down the river with no clue what the outside world looks like anymore. This would be my last chance. *I mistakenly leaned back* and — BAM!

A boulder from the bottom of the river met my face with great force. I saw stars — just like in the cartoons. This was not fun anymore. I pulled the emergency release chord, surfaced gasping, and climbed out of the river. Holding my nose, positive it was bleeding; I rushed back to camp and straight for the bathroom mirror. Luckily no blood, but it was very sore. I'd smashed the upper portion of my nose. A fine dent in the middle of the bridge, which left a flat spot, but from the side it appeared as a lovely bump. *WONDERFUL.*

To my dismay, my beautiful American beak now looked more full-PERSIAN than ever before.

Iranian women often approach me after my comedy shows saying they like it because it looks so masculine.

Translation:

> *"I'm so glad your nose is uglier than mine!"*

Ironically, if I were to have a kid with one of these women, the child would come out with an ugly nose which everyone would assume came from me, when in reality it was the mother's fault! We simply can't have that. With that said, I now have a consultation to have mine fixed... Plus my septum has deviated, and I'm having trouble breathing. For those who think it's fine and I should just leave it, you don't understand. This is a medical emergency and I *have* to do it.

CHAPTER 8: LAW SCHOOL DEFERMENT

After graduating, most people enjoy their summer, celebrate, and relax. Instead, I spent long hours studying for the LSATs to get into law school. I then applied and soon a letter from my number one choice, University of Nevada Las Vegas, came back to me — I had been ACCEPTED! *(One step closer to Persian.)*

My family was proud. I was excited to start, but I also had just begun standup comedy, which was a tough gig, but it was also an interesting path I was on. I decided I would take a one-year deferment and see what happened with standup first. If there was a sign, *any sign* from the universe that I should be in comedy, it had better reveal itself in that deferment year, otherwise, it was straight to law school for me.

Putting that one-year limit on my dream job may have been just what I needed because it forced me to put the pedal to the metal. I tried to improve my standup. Mingle. Network with people. I landed a small TV appearance but that wasn't enough to give up on law school. I made some great connections, and then I met Maz Jobrani.

For those who don't know, Maz Jobrani is the most famous Full-Persian comedian in the world. He has made countless sitcom appearances, starred in several comedy specials, and even acted opposite of Sean Penn and Nicole Kidman on the big screen. He is the Persian George Lopez. The Iranian Chris Rock. Or as Sam Tripoli, a comedian friend of ours, puts it,

> "Maz Jobrani is the Persian Elvis...*He is PELVIS!*"

The first time I saw Maz on stage, I was blown away. After the show, I told him how funny he was and that his occupation was a goal of mine. I found out he was also, at one time, part of a Ph.D. program and made the tough call to take the leap into standup. Because of that faith in himself, he was enjoying a lot of success. Best of all, he proved with hard work, it was attainable.

It was getting close to crunch time for me. Which way was I to go? Say goodbye to comedy and focus on law...or give it all up for the road less traveled?

Then two things happened; I landed another TV spot, and Maz asked me to join him on his tour. We would soon travel to every major city in North America and overseas. I timidly sent a letter to UNLV thanking them for the opportunity but telling them I had to pass on law school. That letter was not easy to write. It was not easy to mail. And it was not easy to share the decision with family. *(My heart rate is increasing just having to relive this memory now.)*

At the time I had only five minutes of mediocre jokes *(some would argue, not much has changed)* and the smallest thread of hope that I was making the right call. When taking a leap to pursue a dream, it is not always clear if there is even a path waiting for you on the other side. But here is where having a non-traditional Iranian dad was key. He wasn't a lawyer or doctor so luckily for me the bar was nice and low. THANKS, DAD!

(If you are wondering why I'm not more successful — it is because, I too am keeping the bar nice and low for my future children as well. It is a family tradition at this point, and the right thing to do.)

It had been decided, I was not going to law school and Dad wasn't happy about it. How do I know? Because he *framed the acceptance letter.* It has remained on display back home as a visual reminder of how successful I almost could have been!

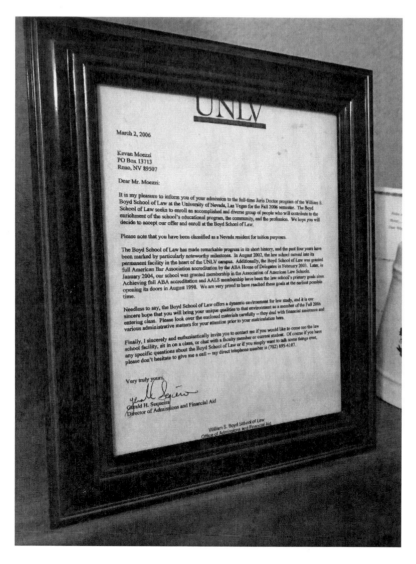

Law School Acceptance

THE MARVELOUS MR. MAZ JOBRANI

When I perform at Persian functions, I often start by saying,

> "The most famous Persian comedian in the world is Maz Jobrani. You all wanted him tonight, but you couldn't afford him. Therefore, you're stuck with me. *Half* as Persian, *half* as funny...but the good news...I'm *half* the price."

That invokes a big applause because it's real, funny, plus if there's something a Persian crowd loves, it's knowing they got a discount.

Maz is truly a pioneer in the community. I've been lucky enough to call him a friend for over a decade. He's helped a countless number of people in the industry over the years. When he asked me to go on tour with him I was ready to jump for joy. This was not a deal to pass up. I was getting upgraded from performing in the back of pizza parlors to the biggest and best comedy clubs in the nation. I went from getting paid in chicken wings to actual U.S. currency. What's not to love?

"Opening" comedians or "Feature Acts" typically go out and warm up the crowd for the headliner. They produce a little buffer as people arrive late, order drinks and otherwise get settled. The crowd is definitely not there to see you, and some evenings they make that more obvious than others. In the end, there was no pressure, because even if it did go poorly, Maz would be on stage to save the show soon enough. On those nights my relationship with the audience was like a standoff with playground bullies.

> "Oh, yea. You may not like *me*, but soon
> my comedy big brother is gonna be up here
> and then you'll be sorry."

A few months into the tour, I got into the groove. I had finally built up to a strong fifteen minutes on stage. The crowd response was becoming more favorable, and the word was getting out "not to miss that first guy."

I was lucky enough to perform with Maz for over three years across several countries. He introduced me to new fans in every major city, and I started getting booked on my own.

As comedians tour, they often swap out who they work with every few years. The day had come; it was time for me to go off on my own.

One problem with going solo: the shows weren't quite as glamorous anymore. The crowds weren't quite as enthused. The venues weren't quite as nice, and the pay wasn't quite as good. It was *quite* the fall from grace.

Plus, I didn't have my comedy big brother to fall back on anymore. If a show went south, it was all on my shoulders.

Another small caveat: instead of fifteen minutes, I was required to take the stage for *fifty* minutes. That is a big jump in maintaining the crowd's attention. There is no shortcut around this phase. You just have to power through it, sometimes fall flat on your face, go home, rewrite, cross your fingers, and hope the next show you don't screw up as bad. *(All, while knowing you're still probably going to screw up just as bad next time.)* That's why when you see an established comedian, they come off so confident. They've been there, done that, and have the battle scars to prove it.

How is it that comics are not nervous when public speaking is most people's biggest fear? Well, because we do it every single night *(sometimes four shows per evening)*. We have made people laugh at noon in Ohio and at 2am in Hollywood. We've done comedy for conventions full of cops and in bowling alleys full of criminals. I've even had to send my jokes to government officials in other countries for approval before I could tell them. Which brings me to Dubai.

DUBAI, DON'T BUY

One of my last major international trips I took with Maz Jobrani was to the Middle East. And I wasn't kidding about getting approval for each joke we told; we actually had to type out our material and send it to the *Standards & Practices* department of the United Arab Emirates prior to arrival. Apparently they needed to look over the stories of my dad in his underwear and our Costco hijinks to make sure it didn't violate any laws. They then set up a phone call to go over it all. This felt like the equivalent of being sent to the principal's office.

The phone call came in from a faceless government official. I answered.

> "We have received your jokes. Is this all of them?"

> "Yes, your excellency."

"You don't have to call me that. And this is
what you will do on stage?"

"Yes...your...sir-ness?"

"Well, I don't know if these jokes will work
for you...however it breaks no laws. You
are free to say these things on stage."

And with that, he hung up.

Umm, "Don't know if the jokes will work?" You have to
hear how I SAYYYYY THE JOKES your royal jerkness!

*(Actually, I can't remember if it was a call or an email,
but that is how I play it back in my head, so we will go
with this version of the story.)*

I had never flown more than six hours in my life and
this haul would be over fifteen. We only had to be there
for two days, but the other comedians suggested we all
extend our trip an extra ten days so we could really
explore the region. That seemed a little excessive to me,

"How about ONE extra day?"

They gasped,

"Are you kidding? Dude make it ten days
to truly experience it or you're going to
regret it. You *have* to!"

I compromised, making my trip a total of five days,
hoping they wouldn't be too upset that I'd bail halfway
through. Upon landing, the other comedians revealed
they all decided to fly home immediately after the show
in order to save money. *MORONS!* And that is how I
ended up spending three days alone in Dubai.

First, let's talk about the shows. The opening show was held in a theater attached to an amazing mall. The mall was so big it had a downhill skiing slope inside covered in actual snow. *No, I'm not kidding.* I repeat — a man-made hill of snow with a chairlift under a glass bubble in the desert so that you can work on your turns.

The food court was not your typical "Hot Dog on a Stick" and "Auntie Anne's Pretzels." They were fine dining restaurants with over twenty forms of cuisine to choose from.

Our show was in a 1000-seat theater and it was sold out.

After performing in the Middle East, it is hard to be nervous about a comedy show in the United States. Most comedians will never know how hard it is to make a woman laugh as she sits there covered from head to toe.

Comedians are trained to look for facial feedback and expressions, but here many of the ladies outfits prohibited that. All we got from some was an eye slit to try and gauge how we were doing. I am not making fun of the ensemble. I am simply saying — that extra layer of clothing added an extra layer of difficulty for me as well. *How would I know when they were laughing?* I decided to hone in on the eyebrows for clues.

After the show, I was confronted with new cultural challenges as well. Many of these fans had awaited our arrival for months. They'd seen all our videos online and wanted a picture. In America, when someone wants a photo you put your arm around them and smile. I went to do this and heard shrieks. I was immediately reprimanded,

"You don't touch! You are not their husband!"

I didn't know what to do with my hands. I decided to just stand up straight and put my arms across my own chest. They approved of this. Many nodded and smiled that I was such a good boy and a quick learner. Looking back at all those pictures, it appears like I'm resting peacefully in a coffin. *Which, from the looks I was getting, is where I'd end up if I kept putting my arms around the women!*

The shows went well and all the comics headed home... except for me.

3 LONELY DAYS IN DUBAI

Sounds like the title of a romance novel. What the hell was I going to do in a foreign country with no friends for three days? Luckily in a place like Dubai, the options were endless.

DAY 1:

After talking to the locals, I discovered Iran is only sixty miles across the Persian Gulf. I could swim! I headed to the beach and put my feet in the water but ultimately decided against it. It's illegal to just swim across borders out there *(and I didn't have any cucumbers to accompany me on the salty journey)*.

To my left, I noticed that amazing hotel that looks like a large sail coming out of the water. You've probably seen photos of it, the famous Burj Al Arab Jumeirah, the most luxurious hotel in the world. One of the people that came to our show had mentioned he was a manager there, so I made my way to the property. As I got closer, I noticed the hotel had a helicopter pad to pick up guests, along with a fleet of brand new Bentleys for those that didn't feel like flying.

The front desk could have thrown me out, but instead paged the hotel manager who greeted me and was kind enough to give me a tour of the nicest room they offered, the Royal Suite. At a starting price of around $24,000 per night, it has hosted kings, queens, presidents, and celebrities from around the world. Tanx God they comp'd my short visit! Had they not, I might still be making payments on it.

Burj Al Arab Jumeirah Hotel

DAY 2:

I toured the other major mall in Dubai, which from what I understand, is somehow bigger than the first. Once you walk outside you can feast your eyes upon the Burj Khalifa, which at 163 floors, had just been crowned the tallest building in the world. That was the one Tom Cruise was able to climb in the Mission Impossible movie. *(I was not given the same clearance.)* There was also a mysterious fire in the building that started the day I was there, which made me nervous. It turned out to be nothing serious but caused quite a stir and not something you want to think about when all alone in the Middle East!

DAY 3:

I was running out of *Dirhams ($)* fast, but there was still one thing I wanted to do. I made a reservation and hopped in a cab heading for the "Swim with the Dolphins" experience at the Atlantis Hotel.

Clouds were rolling in and a storm began. I arrived to find all the other guests had canceled. Apparently, they didn't want to deal with the rainy weather, which made no sense to me. These are dolphins, what the hell do they care if it's RAINING!

Turns out, this was the best thing that could have happened. Usually, it is eight people per dolphin but that day I had my OWN.

And normally there are so many rules:

- Do this.
- Don't do that.
- Touch the dolphin like this.
- Don't ever touch the dolphin like that.

With the low turnout, they threw the rules out,

> "You know what, do whatever you want with the dolphin. Have fun."

I briefly considered putting my thumb in the blowhole but knew the dolphin would probably say,

> "Nuh-uh. Nuh-uh!"

As an animal lover myself, I decided to follow the posted rules anyway.

After that it was time to return home. I realized how happy I was I'd stayed the extra days as I hopped on a plane and waved "bye-bye" to Dubai.

GAZ-PLOSION

While in Dubai, I purchased a box of Gaz, the Iranian nougat candy with pistachios embedded in it. This candy is a favorite, hard to find in the USA and I thought it would make a nice gift for my aunt, Ameh Shirin. After all, it came from a country only sixty miles from Iran and was as close to authentic as I could get. It came in a lovely gold box with Persian writing all over it. The candy is packed in flour so that it doesn't stick to the other pieces and retains its freshness.

All that is great, but I forgot one important detail, I had to go through customs with this item. Sure enough, as I approached the U.S. Border Patrol desk, the officer asked if I brought any items or gifts back with me. I answered truthfully. I held it up and now all this Persian writing looked suspiciously like the ISIS flag. Never noticed that before. His eyes narrowed.

"What is that?"

"Oh, this is just candy."

My voice shaking a bit, now feeling guilty for no reason,

"Just candy? Open it..."

"Oh, I don't think I should open it because..."

"OPEN IT..."

I reluctantly pulled off the lid and — POOF! A cloud of white powder floated into the air. My eyes widened as I considered how this must have looked. It looked like cocaine. It looked like heroin. *It looked like anthrax. It looked like anything other than candy.*

Luckily, the border agent wasn't concerned and waved me right through. Phew, that was close! My next brush with authority wouldn't go quite so smoothly. It was in a different city, on a different trip, and it went a little something like this...

PACKING HEAT

Sitting in an interrogation room surrounded by authorities is quite the predicament, and yet here I was...

On most trips, I usually take my suitcase, but I was going on a short one and my father encouraged me to take his small red duffel bag, since it would be easier to haul around.

I filled it with the bare necessities; one pair of underwear, jeans, a t-shirt, a toothbrush and off to the airport I went.

Packing light allowed me to skip baggage check. I walked directly to security, placed my belongings on the x-ray machine and waltzed through the metal detector with ease.

While waiting on the other side, I noticed something had caught the eye of the TSA agent. He worked furiously on his little controls. I stood there thinking,

> "Ah, must have found something in the bag of that weird guy who went through right before me...I knew he couldn't be trusted."

At this point, the officer frantically waved over a supervisor,

> "I GOT ONE!!!"

I was impressed. Apparently, the TSA found someone trying to smuggle something dangerous onto an airplane. Bad news for that creep/good news for America! I was proud of our country. Thank goodness we have our "boys in light blue" at the front lines.

More agents now huddling around the monitor. Pointing. Deliberating. *Stopping terror.* Watching these experts work was awe-inspiring. I didn't even care that it took a few minutes out of my day; I had a front row seat as they caught a bad guy.

The agent reached in and pulled a bag from the machine,

"Does this *red duffel bag* belong to anyone?

What?!... This must be some mistake! There's hardly *anything* in that bag, let alone a threat to our nation. Had my underwear set off an overly sensitive alarm? *(Remind me to switch detergents.)* Was I being targeted by my Persian last name due to inherent racism and bigotry? Sure, the bag belongs to my Middle Eastern father, but he's a very good natured dude. He's never talked of "Jihad" or uttered "Death to all Infidels" in all the years I've known him *(except for when I didn't go to law school).*

The supervisor firmly stated we couldn't discuss the matter out in the open, and I was taken to the room. THE ROOM! The one we all hear about. The walls were bare. A metal table sat in front of me, the bag in question resting between the agent and me. I was flanked by two scrawny teenage officers doing their best to look menacing.

The questioning began:

"What are your plans?"

"Who were you going to visit?"

"Why are you at the airport?"

As a member of the SAE fraternity, I've been in trouble many times before, but this seemed different. I begged them to tell me what the problem was.

They reached into the bottom of the bag, pulled out a small bullet that had been trapped under the stitching, and held it up to the light,

> "What is *THIS* doing in here?"

It was a .22 caliber bullet, about the length of your pinky nail. Made sense, because my father is licensed by the Sheriff's Department to carry a handgun in Nevada and goes to the shooting range often. Must have fallen out and been trapped there for years.

But before I could explain, it was time for more questions...

> "You do know it's illegal to bring artillery on a flight?"

> "*Artillery?* Isn't that a little extreme? Rambo had *artillery.* I didn't even know that was in there..."

> "You should know what's in any bag before you bring it on the plane."

> "Okay, but it was an accident! My Dad is a cowboy. We have bullets all over our home... he could have one in the bottom of his shoe right now and wouldn't even know it."

Note to self: Remind Dad to check his shoes when I get home.

> "Well just this once we'll make an
> exception but you will be put on the list."

> "*THE* LIST?!?! NO, please don't do that
> sir! I'm very sorry...but I certainly do not
> want to be on ANY lists, let alone *the list*!"

Despite my plea, they took my ID, typed something into a computer, and with that — I was officially put on "The List." While this is happening, I'm struggling with the logic. Sure, they found a .22 bullet but it's not like they found a *gun*. What was my plan — hold everyone on the plane hostage? With such a small weapon, the demands would have to be equally minuscule.

> "OKAY, LISTEN UP, this is a bullet, I will
> throw this at your face, so don't test me. I
> have a list of demands: I want a window
> seat, I want somebody to shut that baby
> up, and I want more of those tasty pretzels
> or else...YOU HEAR ME!?!?"

I snapped out of it as they handed my I.D. back informing me I was free to go. Now extremely late, I sprinted toward my plane. *(Why is it whenever you're in a rush, your plane is at the furthest gate in the entire airport?)* I must have looked more suspicious than ever to the people on that flight. The guy who was in *the room*, with the TSA, and now on *the list* had plopped down in the seat next to them, panting, and above all...sweating bullets.

CHAPTER 9:
THE GODS MUST BE
CRAZY

Just when I feel like I've seen it all…

I've been heckled across three continents, in four languages, by five different genders! *(One for each finger.)* Nobody's got range like me, baby.

By far the most difficult crowds to navigate are the strict religious groups. You are always at risk of crossing an imaginary line you didn't even know existed.

I once performed for the "Druze." Yes, you read that right. Not the Jews, but the Druze — an ancient religion from the Middle East. At this particular event, I found the women to be the most gorgeous I've ever seen. You think I'm kidding? Amal Clooney (George's wife) is reported to come from this faith, so picture a banquet hall full of single women who make the gorgeous Amal look like the "ugly friend." My neck hurt from swiveling so many times that I'm in talks with an attorney as to whether or not there's a potential lawsuit there. Meanwhile, the men at the event were *hideous.*

Flirting with the gals and trying to get a conversation started, I noticed some incredibly ugly men standing casually against the wall, pointing, and laughing at my attempts. One approached me,

>"They are very beautiful, yes?"

I agreed. He then dropped some knowledge,

>"They will never date you."

>"How do you know?"

>"Because you are not Druze. These women only date other Druze like us. If they do not marry Druze they are thrown out of the religion."

I protested,

>"Well, then I will become Druze."

He scoffed,

>"In order to be Druze, you must already be Druze. You cannot convert."

Well, isn't that a convenient little system you have there?! You know how women sometimes say,

>"I wouldn't date him unless he was the last guy on earth?"

Well, this was them! And these hobgoblins were keeping the beautiful women all to themselves under the guise of letting down their entire people and being excommunicated. I'd never heard of such a thing. These princesses were being held as social hostages and wouldn't even let me rescue them if I tried. No wonder the men were so confident *and yet so very unattractive.*

*It is important to note the Druze population has been

dwindling for the last 1,000 years. Well, you know what they say, "You Druze, You Lose."

There are other things I've learned along the way as well. While performing at a Singles Event in a Jewish Temple, I launched into the portion of my act where I make fun of dancing. This usually kills but on this night I got nothing. It wasn't until *after* busting out those incredibly sweet moves I was informed that dancing is strictly forbidden in a temple and they could not believe I dared to do such a thing. I apologized but was still yelled at by a rabbi for longer than the average Bar Mitzvah takes.

Or there was that time an Islamic group hired me to perform at an outdoor festival. It went well for twenty-five minutes. I did one-liners, told stories, made fun of myself, and dazzled them. All was going swimmingly, until suddenly my show ended with getting booed off stage. Talk about a whiplash moment. It was ONE JOKE. And it went something like this...

"You guys have been great. Before I get out of here, I just read in the news there's a Muslim woman suing because they won't let her lifeguard in her burka. Now, I'm all for equal rights but maybe this <u>one</u> job is not for her.

Look, if I'm drowning I want David Hasselhoff's glistening body headed my way in the <u>smallest speedo possible</u>.

But a burka? All that extra fabric Come on. That's a LOTTTTT OF DRAG. Slows her down, plus if she gets tired, now we got two victims in the water!

And who's gonna give mouth-to-mouth!
She'll be like, 'Sorry, you're not my
husband!'"

And with that, I prepared to take a final bow, basking in applause for cleverly presenting the perils of a cultural clash through the art of humor.

What came next was quite the opposite. The show definitely ended there with people making their way to the exit in silence.

Walking to my car, some crazed religious extremist *(who would define himself as a "moderate," I'm sure)* caught up with me. He looked young; a student, maybe about twenty years old, and he grabbed my arm proceeding to tell me how upset he was on behalf of his entire faith. Spit flew from his mouth as he shouted,

"HOW...DARE YOU...DO YOU KNOW HOW YOU DISRESPECT? THESE VOMEN RISK THEIR LIVES TO VEAR BURKA."

"Look, man, it was a thirty-minute show. That was one joke. What did you think of the other twenty-five? Seemed okay to me."

He was now shaking, eyes filled with rage,

"SEEMED OKAY?! YOU TINK THAT OKAY??? YOU KNOW YOUR PROBLEM. YOUR JOKES ARE ANTI-ISLAMIC!"

"Dude, that joke was about swimming. It was not anti-Islamic, if anything it was *HYDRODYNAMIC!*"

(Imagine had I informed him how many cucumbers one could fit in a burkini!)

I shook him off my arm, and he stormed off. But then I thought about his words. I focused on what he was trying to say. I considered the deeper message. And after intense reflection I realized...*I still don't want a lifeguard wearing extra clothing. Now if you'll excuse me I'm going to try and find me a Druze.*

BI-POLAR PERSIANS

Iranians as a group have a wide range of beliefs, opinions, and political views. It is impossible to pigeonhole how they'll feel about any issue. In fact, ask ten Iranians their political opinions and you will get *sixteen different answers!* Here's why we are such a complex group of individuals:

Iranians are from the Middle East...
But not considered Arab like many of their neighbors.

Iran was once an open society...
But is currently controlled by a strict religious regime.

Some Iranians love their home country...
But some fled their home country.

Iranians are immigrants who understand the minority plight. Socially; they tend to lean "LEFT"...
But they are largely well-off, so fiscally they tend to lean "RIGHT."

Iranians are often considered "brown people" by Westerners...
But they will tell you they are the original Caucasians from the caucus region of Asia.

...and the list goes on. No wonder we get so confused!

CHAPTER 10: PERSIAN PARTIES

If you are going to hang with Persians you are going to attend a lot of parties. Here are a few helpful hints if you happen to receive an invite to any Middle Eastern cultural event, wedding, fundraiser, or extravaganza.

THE ART OF COMING AND GOING

#1. How to Dress

The invitation almost never tells you how to dress *(because you are supposed to already know)*. T-shirt and jeans are never on the menu. If they say "casual" and you show up casual, you will be underdressed. Even if they claim it's a pool party; show up in dress pants, dress shirt, designer sports coat, and fancy shoes. You can get in the pool in that if you need to.

If they say "fancy," then you may want to take out a second mortgage on your home. You have some shopping to do.

The women will be wearing a new outfit for every occasion. Never a repeat! Do not be intimidated by this. Know that some of them keep the tags and will be returning the clothes to Bloomingdale's the next day. If you ever wonder how a "Versace" ended up at "TJ MAXX" there's a good chance it's because a Persian returned it after an event. *(It also may smell like kabob.)*

Of course I'm kidding, very few people would actually do this. However, I've had people pull me aside to reveal they've driven two towns over so as to anonymously return items to a store without being recognized by any friends.

#2. Show Up Late

For any social occasion, if you're late, you're actually on time. If you're on time — you're early. And if you're early — you're going to be the only one sitting there! If the invite says 7pm and you show up at 7pm, prepare to twiddle your thumbs for an hour.

#3. Valet Parking

Parking will be a breeze because there's always "valet" *(even for a small house party)*. A teenager in a vest who just obtained his learning permit is ready to take your new car and park it half in a ditch 100-yards away... something you could have easily done yourself.

Also, be careful when picking up your car to leave. I once saw a valet bring up a brand new white BMW with no license plates. The owner gave a tip, got in his vehicle, and drove off. Just then another white BMW pulled up. It too had no license plates. The guy went to get in, looked closely, and freaked out,

> "This isn't mine??? WAIT! THAT ONE
> WAS MINE?!!"

Realizing there had been a mix-up, four valets sprinted down the block frantically waving their arms for the older man in the first car to stop.

To everyone's relief the brake lights came on and the guy backed all the way up. Laughing about it, the two owners hugged, swapped to their rightful vehicles, complimented each other on their taste in cars, and drove off.

I joked with the valet,

> "Wow, isn't that something! What are the odds?"

Valet:

> "That's the fourth time it's happened this week."

Rest assured, this would never happen to me. In my car I keep dirty clothes, receipts, and trash to clearly indicate its rightful owner and now tell women this is merely a safety precaution.

#4. Leaving on Time...

If you want to *LEAVE* a Middle Eastern event on time, you need to start saying "goodbye" WHEN YOU ARRIVE.

Most parties you can shout your goodbyes to the host from across the lawn and they'll wave right back.

Middle Eastern goodbyes take forever. You must go to every guest at the party, compliment them and kiss them on both cheeks — the husband, the wife, the three kids. *(If you start kissing the dog, you may have gone too far.)* By the time you get to the last person at the party, the first family will exclaim,

> "You're still here? Come say goodbye one more time!"

Then, prepare to start the whole process all over again.

#5. Getting Everyone to Leave Your Party...

If you throw a party and Persians come, they will never leave.

Because of that, I give you this simple announcement to vacate everyone at once. Simply read this aloud...

> "Will the owner of a white Mercedes-Benz, please go outside...Your car is being towed.

Works every time. For the remaining people in the room...

> "*AND* the owner of a white BMW...

#6. Don't Show Up At All:

If you have an event and invite Middle Eastern people, they will always confirm they will attend. That does not mean they are actually coming. In their mind, it would be rude to say no. Therefore the answer is "Yes, I'll be there. ABSOLUTELY." Then if needed, they'll come up with a way to get out of it later.

I've had many events where I invited Persians who promised to come. I bought all the decorations, reserved the venue, and set out all the food. The day of the event, the messages started rolling in one-by-one. Would you believe, *everyone* was having a "family emergency?" All these separate families experiencing different "family emergencies" all at the same time?! This must be big. What could it be; earthquake, gas line explosion, anthrax dust filling the air, or perhaps a combination of all three? I rushed to the TV. Surely a calamity of this magnitude would be on the news. Yet, to my surprise, there was no coverage of any emergencies anywhere.

Long ago Persians discovered that two magic words are the perfect excuse out of any obligation: "family" which we all love, and "emergency" which we can all understand.

As the host, instead of being *mad* at them for flaking, *you are now the one that has to apologize!* Never mind all the planning, time, and money you spent. Somehow they have now become the victims in all of this. *Very clever indeed.*

You don't want to call anyone a liar, but I can assure you, if every single "family emergency" were real, there'd be no one alive today in the Middle East. That's just way too many emergencies for one culture to survive.

PERSIAN WEDDINGS

Persian weddings rank quite high on the opulence scale. When done to the fullest, they can last three days. Books have been written on the art of the Persian wedding. From me, you will only get the *comedian's abridged version.*

Early on in my comedy career, I was asked to perform at a Persian wedding. This was the first time I'd ever seen one, let alone told jokes there. I'm happy to say, it went well enough that I've performed at many more since.

The first one I attended had an estimated price tag of $400,000 and looked like something Walt Disney might have dreamt up himself; complete with fountains, ballroom gowns, and drone cameras capturing the engagement from coastal views. As I looked around, I noticed nobody had canceled on this event due to "family emergency."

This was night two of a three-day affair. The wait staff, appetizers, food, and ceremony were all impeccable. It was then my turn to take the stage. *No pressure.*

There is a certain science to setting up a room for standup comedy. Look closely and notice comedy clubs have mastered this, featuring their talent in the most ideal conditions. Things like a small dark room, two-drink minimum, a spotlight on the comedian, and a clear sounding microphone are a must. Having strangers sit elbow-to-elbow also helps. It makes it so that even if you don't personally find a joke funny, the reaction from the couple next to you makes a world of difference. As I'm sure you've heard before; laughter *is* contagious.

On the opposite end of that spectrum is a wedding reception. A cavernous hall, a 2,000 square-foot dance floor between the stage and audience, and big round tables *(which encourage talking)* are not ideal. Oh, and for an extra level of difficulty, let's throw in some older folks who think it's inappropriate to have a comedian telling jokes at a wedding.

This is what I was up against. The DJ made a muffled announcement, no one heard it, and before anyone was quiet, handed me the microphone. I tried to capture everyone's attention, and it wasn't easy.

The first couple minutes involved getting the crowd settled. It worked. Then I noticed some jokes were landing. Finally, I found my groove.

"After seeing this venue, I realize I probably should have charged a lot more."

LAUGH

"I noticed none of the women are laughing tonight. They're too busy trying to figure out how to steal the beautiful centerpieces without getting caught!"

BIG LAUGH

Pointing to the table of single bridesmaids I made an impromptu announcement that I didn't need to be paid at all.

"FORGET MONEY. Let's do this the traditional way. Just give me one of these ladies, two goats, and we'll call it even!"

BIGGER LAUGH

With that, I locked arms with the cute girl laughing the hardest and walked out the side door, waving goodbye to everyone in the room.

ROUND OF APPLAUSE

After a few moments, we re-entered the room and people were *still laughing*. Well, everyone except her dad.

(Sadly, in the end, he did not agree to the offer. I had to return her and was paid for my time in cash. I probably should have negotiated a little harder.)

Since then, I've performed at several weddings for people of all cultural backgrounds. Word gets around and not many comics are "killing it" on the wedding circuit, as you can imagine.

Not long after that night, an Indian couple booked me to perform at their nuptials. Indian? Sure. Some of my Persian jokes would work because the cultures are similar, but I wanted to make sure this was a hit. I looked at the old show, "The Newlywed Game" for guidance.

That night, the performance began with five minutes of my standard jokes. I then brought out two chairs, placed the couple in the middle of the dance floor, and made them my victims for the final portion of my act. The audience was suddenly more engaged now that the two people they all came to see were part of the show.

I had interviewed each separately before the reception asking about their favorite foods, movies, ice creams, etc. I then asked them what their partner might answer for those exact questions.

As suspected, they had conflicting answers, and where there is conflict, there is comedy! The more *"off"* their responses were, *the better.*

In the middle of the dance floor, I revealed all of the inconsistencies.

To the groom,

> "I asked you, 'What is her favorite movie.' You thought it was, *Terminator.* She said *TITANIC!*
>
> ...both James Cameron movies but you blew it man."

BIG LAUGHS

To the bride,

> "I asked, 'What is his favorite thing to do for fun.' You said, *Go to the museums with you.* He said, *SLEEP...* And, he didn't even add the *'with you'* part!

HUGE LAUGHS

This couple was professionally successful. I found out she was becoming an eye doctor and he was a practicing urologist *(my dad would've been proud).*

So, for my final joke, I made up a little historical account of their early years,

"It's obvious that the bride would become
an eye doctor one day. Her parents told me
as a teenager she spent many nights in
front of the mirror perfecting her eyebrows
and lashes. That part of her body was once
her passion, and now it is her profession."

Putting a hand on the groom's shoulder,

"And he's a urologist...so, we all know
what he was doing as a teenager all those
years!"

PEOPLE FELL OUT OF THEIR CHAIRS

His buddies said they'd be re-using that joke for years.

Two people that can laugh together during serious
occasions like this will definitely last. Each time I'm
invited to perform at a wedding, it's an honor to be a part
of their celebration.

The typical Persian wedding does not have a comedian.
Instead they take an entirely different approach in a
tradition known as "The Wedding Knife Dance." This
one took me by surprise, but some receptions will have
a ceremonial dance where someone from the bride's side
steals the knife during the cutting of the cake. She then
dances for several minutes all around the groom wielding
this deadly object. He must throw money at her to try and
get the knife back. She collects the bills but hands the
knife to another friend who does the same thing. Soon he
is out of money. Eventually the bride takes the knife last,
waves it in his face a few times for good measure before
finally cutting the cake. As a guy, the implied message
behind this act is received loud and clear!

JUST (GET) MARRIED!

A Persian grandmother's last job on earth is to make sure the young women in her family get married off. These grandmothers will always give advice whether anyone is asking them for it or not. It usually goes something like this...

AGE: UNSOLICITED ADVICE:

20   *You need to find a nice Persian boy and get married.*

25   *You need to find a nice Middle Eastern boy and get married.*

30   *You need to find a boy and get married already.*

35+   *YOU NEED TO MARRY SOMEBODY. Anybody. Does not have to be nice. Does not need to be Middle Eastern. Does not even have to be a boy. I see that Ellen on TV and even she got married.*

Ironically, our conservative grandmas become more liberal the OLDER *her unmarried family members* get!

MEETING FAMILY: STAGES 1-6

Our culture once had arranged marriages; the parents acted as high-powered agents, handling the intricate details of eternal matrimony. Two people that didn't know each other would be married by 21 and stay together until death did them part. They'd even toss a few farm animals into the deal to sweeten the pot. NOT ANYMORE.

We foolishly decided to take matters into our own hands thinking we could do a better job conducting the negotiations ourselves. The results have been disastrous. With everyone acting as a free agent, most of us remain undrafted. Lonely, furiously swiping our phones in pursuit of love well into our 30's. Often divorced by our 40's *(and sadly, no one's getting any farm animals in the process)*. Maybe it's time we apologize and beg our parents to represent us once again before we start settling for even less!

Before I can even think about a wedding, I have to find *the one*. And then I have to introduce *the one* to *the family*. For ethnic people, we have to be careful when bringing a potential mate around, taking special care in considering whom they should meet first. The wrong order can mess up your chances and will have *the one* heading for *the door*.

The correct order is as follows. Notice the natural progression of "crazy," from Level 1-6 with the hopes that *the one* is too committed by then to bail on the relationship. Use this as a general guide for your family as well:

 Brothers, Sisters, and Cousins. *Plus any Normal Americanized fellow halfies.*

 Aunts and Uncles. *Born in Iran, but still pretty cool, friendly and hospitable.*

 Family friends who we *call* cousins *(even though they aren't really related to us).*

*(Then we take a break for a while and check in with
<u>the one</u> to make sure they're still okay with the idea of
potentially joining this family. If "no," repeats steps 1
through 3. If "yes," move to Level 4.)*

2nd Cousins. They are a little weirder but,
hey, *the one* may not notice. *(Visit during
daylight hours only.)*

Parents. But be careful because the
parents will now pressure you about where
your relationship is with *the one* for eternity.

Oldest Uncle who just sits in front of the
TV and yells "ANIMAL!"

Look around. If your loved one is still by your side, this is
a keeper and you must marry them immediately.

There's a **LEVEL 7** as well. These are family members
kept locked away in a basement where they belong,
only permitted to see sunlight two times a week while
supervised. I highly recommend you don't tell *the one*
about any Level 7s until *after* you're married. At that
point what can they say?

"Too late now honey, *they're FAMILY!*"

Mission accomplished!

*If you're reading this with a family member and they ask
which category they fall into on the scale, just be honest
and tell them, "You're a LEVEL 7!"*

NOWRUZ

Nowruz (a.k.a. Persian New Year) is a holiday celebrated by over 300,000,000 around the world in the month of March. Kids get new clothes, gifts, and cash from the adults...and somehow my father NEVER TOLD ME ABOUT IT. *(I think he was trying to save money.)* Now aware of these festivities, I'm in the process of suing him for thirty years of "Back-Holiday-Child-Support."

Of course, this holiday is not about material gifts; rather it's about ushering in the New Year right around the time of the Spring Equinox. It is often credited to the ancient religion of Zoroastrianism and even predates it. This global celebration of food, family, happiness, and Mother Nature is non-religious, non-political, and welcome to all.

As a comedian, one year; I noticed my calendar mysteriously filling up around March. The groups booking me simply assumed I already knew what Nowruz (aka: Nahruz, Nooruz, Navruz, Nouruz, Nooroos) was. *(There are a lot of spellings and I'm now receiving hate mail for missing a few. Allow me to go delete them from my inbox...Okay, back again.)*

Arriving at my first Nowruz event, I realized it looked like a wedding where nobody had to get married. *(Talk about a happy occasion!)* The hotel banquet hall was decked out with fresh fruit and delicious food spanning from one side to the other. Everyone was wearing new outfits *(without the return tags)* and each family showed up with several generations by their side, which is also part of the tradition.

Performers were playing ancient instruments like odd shaped drums and tambourines that appeared to have safety pins dangling off the sides. People were mingling. There was a guy in a red outfit dancing, falling on the floor, chasing the kids around, and tossing candy at them. He wasn't part of the event, so security quickly had him arrested. *KIDDING.*

That's actually a character known as Haji Firuz, the court-jester who brings slapstick laughter to the New Year's party. He usually appears alongside Amoo Nowruz (Uncle New Year) who is a fellow mascot that tosses money to the children. Both are a big hit.

There was a large table near the entrance that can best be described as a Christmas tree, laid out flat. It is called a "haft-seen" which translates to *"7 things that start with 'S.'"* Each item on the table represents something important to keep in mind for the New Year.

Sabze – *Grass - which represents new growth*
Seer – *Garlic - represents medicine*
Sekkeh – *Gold Coins - represents prosperity*
Seb – *Apple - represents beauty*
Serkeh – *Vinegar - represents age/wisdom*
Sumac – *Spice - represents the sunrise*
Senjeh – *Pudding - represents affluence*

*Just for good measure they throw a mirror, a goldfish, and a book of poetry on the table as well.

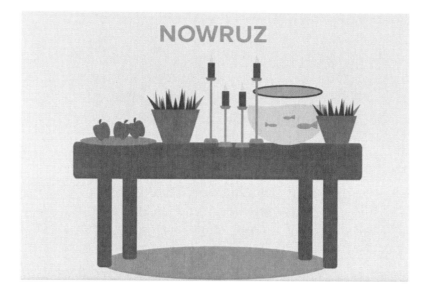

I was trying to take all of this in, but it was overwhelming. It was explained to me several times but the information was coming too fast — too furious. That's when I had an idea. Instead of learning all this by myself, which clearly wasn't working, why not hire a camera crew and invite the viewer to experience these things for the first time as well?

I got to work and began filming my Nowruz tour. We showed every aspect of the holiday including "jumping over fire" which happens the week before Nowruz. Middle Eastern people light these little bonfires in a parking lot, hold hands, and jump over them together. *(So before you call 9-1-1, make sure it is not a bunch of Iranians celebrating the holiday first.)* The fires may look small to you, but our legs are hairy. Plus, we wear a lot of cologne, which makes us extremely flammable. The best part, after we jump over that fire, *we don't have to shave our legs for another year!*

Our last stop was to meet the man, the myth, the legend himself...the IRON SHEIK. Even though he was a few decades into retirement, the cameraman and I were still intimidated by his presence. This explains why all that footage came out a little shaky. We shared stories, laughed, and he gave advice on how to stay focused and in shape while constantly on the road.

> "Persian men get fat because we eat traditional meals but we no longer do traditional work. You can't eat like a sheepherder if you're no longer laboring like one!"

The "bad guy" who used to entertain and frighten me through my TV screen could not have been any nicer. He even autographed a photo for my dad, thanking him for the support back when it could have cost us our life that fateful night at the Lawlor Events Center.

We edited all that footage down to the best 80 minutes and created the award-winning documentary "NOWRUZ: Lost & Found." Not bad for someone who knew nothing about the holiday just a few years earlier.

It warms my heart whenever a Middle Eastern person approaches me saying *even they* learned something new from watching the film. Another comment I've heard repeatedly,

> "My kids weren't that excited about their culture, but your movie made them want to participate this year."

One last piece of advice for anyone planning on attending seventeen Nowruz parties in a year; consider becoming a vegetarian in February, because you will be eating a LOT OF KABOB in the month of March!

DANCING

Persians love to dance and will do so for several hours at any event. I have yet to attend a Persian funeral, but I bet they're working on a way to respectfully add dancing to that, too!

When I perform at Middle Eastern events, there's almost always a huge dance floor between the stage and nearest audience members. I always beg the organizers to bring chairs in closer to the stage so that the presenters can have the undivided attention of the audience. After all, it's hard to shout to people who are 40-feet away.

The organizers always decline my request.

> "We want the crowd to know that there will be dancing later."

For some reason, that wood floor must remain vacant as a beacon, signaling that boogying will eventually take place.

One by one each speaker approaches the podium and gives it their best, inevitably having a hard time with their presentation while Iranians chat, take photos, stand up to greet those walking in late, and generally do everything *other than* listen to the person with the microphone.

Then suddenly the DJ takes over,

> "Ok, time to dance!"

With that, he now has their undivided attention. They pop right out of their chairs and do whatever he asks of them on the dance floor for the next four hours.

Personally, dancing is not really my thing, which is unacceptable to Iranians. To get more familiar with the styles, a little while back I signed up for a Middle Eastern dance class. If I was learning to dance, I wasn't going alone. I convinced two friends to join me by promising to take them out to lunch afterward.

Our gorgeous instructor had years of teaching experience and was an expert in several styles including; Persian, Indian, and even a snake-wielding Belly Dance.

We spent the first hour discussing all the various moves women typically do, and wow, do they have a lot to choose from. They could shimmy, belly roll, dance with swords, toss their hair, move their hips, and wiggle their eyebrows. They're encouraged to make intense eye contact, glide straight toward you, and at the last minute — prance away as a tease. They could hold one arm way up in the air and let it gracefully cascade down to their waist as if to say,

> "I bet you wish you could touch this waterfall...but no, you may not touch this waterfall!"

This was getting exhausting. The lesson was almost done and we hadn't even gone over the "guy moves" yet. Finally, our instructor revealed our choreography. We were instructed to clap our hands for the ladies. *THAT'S IT!* Had I really waited this long for THIS? I was then told we could snap our fingers for them as well. If we really wanted to ramp it up, we could walk around the ladies AS we clapped our hands and snapped our fingers.

But the number one rule: You are not allowed to TOUCH the ladies.

I complained that these were not enough moves, and in the interest of gender equality, we were going to need to some more options. Our instructor thought for a moment and remembered "the light bulb." This was more of an Indian style, but it was something we could do with our hands.

> "Hold them high in the air and pretend to unscrew a light bulb."

That was it. Now every time I go to an event I clap, I snap, I pretend to unscrew the light bulb, and I fit right in.

A final word of advice; always do the "light bulbs" way up high in the air. While dancing with a curvy beauty, I once put my arms straight out, in an attempt to change the "headlights." *Apparently those bulbs do not need any unscrewing.*

Search: "NOWRUZ: LOST & FOUND" to see this and more clips from the award-winning documentary.

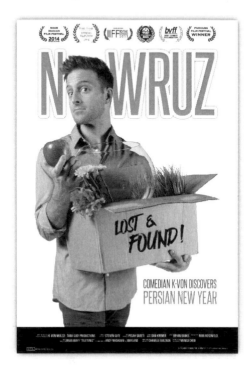

CHAPTER 11: TANX GOD PRODUCTIONS

Other cultures are getting their own mainstream television shows, and we're stuck with "The Shahs of Sunset." We need more positive Iranian role models on TV to better represent our people. Instead of racking our brains trying to dream up new shows, how about a Persian reboot of some old favorites? Here are just a handful I've come up with...

BEVERLY HILLS 90210
➜ *WESTWOOD 90024*

THE PRICE IS RIGHT
➜ *DIS' PRICE IS OUTRAGEOUS*

HOW I MET YOUR MOTHER
➜ *HOW I MET YOUR BABA*

THE FRESH PRINCE OF BEL AIR
➜ *THE PERSIAN PRINCE OF VANCOUVER*

THE WEST WING
➜ *THE VESTWOOD VING*

SAVED BY THE BELL
➜ *SAVED BY THE KABOB*

FRIENDS
➔ *MY FERIEND...*

ARE YOU SMARTER THAN A 5TH GRADER?
➔ *ARE YOU SMARTER THAN A PhD?*

WHO WANTS TO BE A MILLIONAIRE...
➔ *WHO IS ALREADY A MILLIONAIRE...*

DANCING WITH THE STARS
➔ *BELLYDANCING WITH THE STARS*

SO YOU THINK YOU CAN DANCE?
➔ *SO YOU THINK YOU CAN TAROF?*

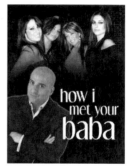

"Excuse me but...

...dis price is outrageous!"

These shows will be good for integrating friendly Iranians into pop culture. Added benefit: with programming like this, Americans will shut off their TV's, head outdoors, and get more exercise for a change!

TEDX TALK

Reno is a great place to be from — a decent sized population with small town appeal. That's how it earned the nickname "Biggest Little City in the World."

Had I been a comedian from somewhere like Chicago, San Francisco, or New York, it would be extremely hard to make my mark in the community. I'd be just another cog in the wheel. However, I'm the only standup comic actually *from RENO (which goes well with "The Most Famous Half-Persian Comedian in the World," I might add)*. So the town has been fantastic for me.

This nice little fact came into play when Reno was set to hold a TEDx Talk. If you don't know what those are check them out online. These hugely popular speeches offer a mind-opening look into a wide array of science, invention, technology, or cultural topics.

The organizers reached out to me to be one of those speakers. I jumped at the opportunity even though I had no idea was I was going to talk about.

Fresh off the "Nowruz" documentary, I knew that was a topic I now had some expertise in. I was relieved after an online search that nothing like that had been done yet. *FANTASTIC!*

The day of the event was very exciting. You want to be a memorable speaker, but each presentation is so diverse and unique it's hard to tell whether yours will be a standout or fall hopelessly flat. I eventually took the stage, and in a blink it was over. Hometown friends said they liked it *but they're kind of obligated to give that kind of feedback.* I took their word for it, we celebrated, and chalked it up as a success.

Six months later, I received the footage and was devastated. Not only did it *come off flat.* I couldn't hear any laughs *(and these were jokes that I knew worked).* And somehow, the camera angle gave me not just a double, but a TRIPLE-CHIN! I put that footage on the shelf and vowed to never share it. *(Something comedians do often.)*

That summer, I was going through some files and stumbled upon the talk. I decided to watch it again. To my surprise, it wasn't *that* bad. Emailing the producers, I asked if they had any other angle other than "up my nostrils" and to my surprise they did! They sent over another clip with an even better audio recording where I could actually hear the audience laughing. With some editing skills I'd acquired over the years, I laid the higher quality sound over the original clip. I then added some insert shots so that when the crowd was laughing, we showed, *get this*, THE CROWD LAUGHING. *A novel idea huh?*

Wouldn't ya know it? This made *all* the difference. I decided to post it online, and the response was fantastic. In no time, it was shared by a few thousand people and climbed to a million views. During the Nowruz holiday, my presentation enjoyed a second bump with people writing in from around the world, saying it was a favorite.

To think it almost never saw the light of day! This taught me that with the magic of editing almost ANYTHING can be fixed. Better yet, it reminded me to deliver it better the first time...oh, and to start doing a lot more chin exercises.

*To view it online, search: "K-von TEDx Talk."

BED & BREAKFAST

Call me a diva, but when I travel I like to stay in a hotel. Starting out, I'd happily crash on couches, in dorm rooms, even rent a car with a big back seat. I've slept on the delightful airport floor more than once. *(Did you know a shoe wrapped in dirty clothes feels remarkably like a pillow if you're tired enough?)*

As an Eagle Scout, I'm not above going back to any of that, however the hotel is preferable. There are people who book me that try to get creative with the accommodations just to save $100.

> "We're on a very tight budget, but a nice older lady in our organization has offered for you to sleep at her house."

I try to explain that I keep weird hours, so perhaps we should shoot for a hotel room instead. After all, at a random person's home, I've discovered it's considered impolite to throw my suitcase on the bed, take off my pants, and start singing as I walk down the hall to shower at two in the morning. The doors at host families' homes never have locks and as you are lying there in your underwear someone will walk right in and say,

"Hope you don't mind I made you some tea. Where shall I put this?"

First of all, nobody asked for tea. Secondly, please pass me that saucer so I can cover myself with it.

It's hard to complain because in reality, it is *their* home and you are *their* guest. But complain I must! Entertainers only have a few hours to take a nap, change, and prepare for a show. Every minute is precious.

In one city, the booker I was staying with woke me up telling me we needed to go meet some of his neighbors. We walked down the street to a backyard barbecue where I was introduced as "the comedian from out of town." I raised my arm to wave hello and was greeted with a water balloon to the crotch. A golden retriever ran between my legs and someone handed me a hot dog. No one at the BBQ had any clue who the hell I was. I asked if any were coming to my comedy show that night, and they unanimously said "no." They couldn't make it since they were going to be tuckered out from the day's festivities. They then asked me to tell a few jokes so they could see if it was something they would have wanted to checkout had they been able to attend.

Another time a booker asked me to stay with his mother and not to worry as I'd have the whole basement to myself. I really didn't want to, but he insisted, saying it would be great. Once I arrived, I realized he had cats hanging out all over the house. My eyes started watering, as I'm highly allergic. He led me down to the basement apologizing,

> "Geez, I wish I would've known. You don't have any medicine for that?"

I don't typically travel with medicine like that because I DON'T TYPICALLY STAY IN BASEMENTS FULL OF CATS. We walked past several litter boxes and scratching posts. As he opened the door to my room, four more felines scurried out. He was apologetic,

> "I feel bad. And this is where the cats normally sleep, too! Remember — keep the door closed or they'll definitely keep coming back in."

As I unpacked, he called for me to please come upstairs. That's where he revealed his mother wanted to meet me, and to please follow him. He led me down a long dark hall and knocked on a door. The person on the other side shouted something in Farsi that sounded a lot like, "Go away!"

He then pushed his way in, leaving me at the door. I could faintly make out the murmurs between him and his mother,

> "Mom, he just wants to come in and meet you."

NO sir. NO *I* did not want to *"come in and meet her."*

In fact I opposed this bedroom summit as much as she did. Exasperation was in her voice,

> "Why he comes here? Dis is bedroom! He has no manners. I don't vant him here."

From the doorway, I could see she was hooked up to various medical equipment *(which seemed to beep louder and faster by the minute). Clearly, this experience was not good for her vital signs.*

> "Mom. He is comedian. He came a long way to see you."

He turned, begging me to come in and start telling some jokes. I tried to mutter out a few one-liners for my fully reclined audience of one, but it was painfully obvious she wasn't enjoying my act. I decided to get out before her heart rate fell as flat as my material.

From that day forward I have deliberately left "Hospice Comedian" off my resume.

These are but a few of the experiences that have made me a hardliner when it comes to demanding my own hotel. I could go on and on with stories just like these. Each time I let my guard down I'm quickly punished for it. The last time this happened was in Boston where I was headed to perform for a Persian New Year event.

The organizers told me I could stay in their apartment. I immediately refused, but, *as usual*, they insisted, promising I'd be the only one staying there. After telling them my previous predicaments, they assured me there'd be no surprises, no cats, and no family members on life support. Reluctantly, I agreed.

Upon arrival, the place was very clean. It overlooked the water and was nicer than a hotel. Perhaps I had been a tad too stubborn with these fine people. They even left a note for me on the coffee table.

> "Make yourself at home. Help yourself to whatever you'd like. There's food in the refrigerator ☺"

I made my way to the kitchen and in true Iranian fashion, the fridge was packed full of watermelon, plums, nectarines, strawberries, and cherries.

How nice of them! I ate as much as I could, wrote some jokes and took a nap. I woke up, finished off the rest of the fruit, and headed to the event. The couple greeted me at the entrance asking if the apartment met my expectations. It did. I thanked them for their hospitality and told them the fruit was a very nice touch but way too much.

> "I almost couldn't finish it all!"

They glanced at each other nervously,

> "You...ate *all* the fruit?"

> "Yes..."

> "We just sent a volunteer to go pick it up. That was meant for the entire party tonight."

Unknowingly I'd deprived about fifty people of their dessert for the evening. While apologetic, in the back of my mind I couldn't help but think..."That's what you get for not offering me a hotel..."

I then spent the rest of the night on their toilet, *which is also what they get for not offering me a hotel*. It was a very good thing for both of us they weren't home.

MERCHANDISE

One way that comedians supplement their income is by selling t-shirts, standup specials, and other merchandise on the road. I love doing this because it also provides an opportunity to do a "meet-and-greet" and connect with your fans after the show. It also serves as an opportunity to get even more comedy material.

The first thing I do is — if there are any well-behaved kids at my all-ages events — I tell them to get over here and help me sell my items. The kids are usually bored and love to have a little job. Plus adults can't just walk by now; they *have* to buy something because of the puppy dog eyes staring back at them. *(An evil tactic I stole from the Girl Scouts.)*

Of course, after they work for me, they get to choose an item off the table and go home with a tip *(plus, a fun memory of hanging with a very cool comedian, I might add)*. A win-win!

Whatever price you attempt to give an item, Middle Eastern people will try to haggle with you. So I warn the kids to be ready for that *(a valuable life lesson)*.

Sometimes people get upset once they get to the merchandise table. Persian women will ask why I don't offer more T-shirt colors, what about tank tops, and have I considered V-necks as well? It seems they forgot that I'm a comedian, not a traveling department store.

We often autograph items as well. In Chicago, a woman

with a very unusual name asked me to sign her shirt. As she said her name I had trouble with it. I'd never heard that one before and asked her to spell it out for me. She rolled her eyes,

> "Are you serious? It's a pretty common name."

I reminded her I'm half-Persian, bad at spelling, and didn't want to ruin her shirt so please bear with me. She sighed and rolled her eyes again, impatiently listing each letter for me,

> "G. H- A... H...Z. H. A...H-L. E...H"

Yup...if you're looking at that a little confused, NOW YOU KNOW HOW I WAS FEELING. How on earth was I supposed to know how to spell that correctly without her help?

As I looked at the name I couldn't help but think,

> "My god, there's a lot of H's. No wonder my dad says 'Tanx God.' There's no more H's left."

We now have a shortage of H's in the Middle East because Ghahzhahleh took them all. In fact, when they play "Wheel Of Fortune" in that part of the world, you can't even buy an H anymore.

I always try to go above and beyond in the meet and greet line. I'll never forget the guy who asked me to sign a DVD for both Iradj and Touraj. Just for good measure, I took my marker and made it out to Threeraj, Fouraj, and Fiveraj as well.

WHAT'S IN A NAME

Some of the most beautiful Persian names unfortunately get lost in translation once they arrive to the West. I will list the more problematic names below so you can see just how bad we have it.

First we start with mine. "K-von" was the name of an ancient god who ruled over the planet Saturn. And then there's "Moezzi"...which means nothing. However, technically "moez" in Persian means "banana." So if someone is very "moez-i" — that's gotta be pretty good, right? Therefore, I suppose my name fully translated is: "THE GOD WHO RULES OVER THE PLANET SATURN WITH A GIANT BANANA."

Negar
This one will get you in trouble. Imagine losing your child in the mall and over the loudspeaker, you hear,

> "We have a Negar here. We can't find this Negar's parents. I repeat, does anyone know this Negar?"

Or if she won't get in the car, you may find yourself standing in the parking lot screaming,

> "Negar, PLEASE!"

Rambod and Arash
Both are men's names. If you're not careful and *"Ram"* your *"bod"* too much, you might end up with "A-rash."

Bahman
Get ready for every kid to sing the Caped Crusader's theme song when this guy comes around...

"Nana nana nana nana — *BAH MAN!*"

Borzoo
Where do "boars" belong? In a "zoo" of course.

Hooshang
Sounds like someone with a lateral lisp..."*Hoo shang*" that *shong* I jusht heard on shoundcloud? Does anyone know *hoo shang* it?

Fardad
I used to have a close dad, but then he moved away...

Mansoor
Man and sewer should never go together.

Goli
It's not just a name; it's a soccer position as well.

Kobra
Is this the name of a Persian girl or a WWE Wrestler?

Poopak and Pooneh
These are just a few of the *"Poo-names"* but there are others. As a general rule: Poo, Poop, and/or Poon should never be in an American name if it can be avoided.

Darya
This sounds like what happens when you eat too much Persian stew. You get Darya...

Oldooz
A girl's name. Some ladies like young dudes, while others prefer *Oldooz*.

Nazi
A fun and funky name for a woman, if only it weren't for that whole World War II "thing"...

Last Names

If you think the first names are bad, you ain't seen nothin' yet. The last names are even worse! I'll spare you the hundreds of examples and provide you with just one. Know that this Iranian weightlifter had the longest last name in all of the Olympics.

Saeid Mohammadpourkarkaragh

Try saying that five times fast. Just rolls off the tongue, doesn't it? It's a good thing he has those big wide shoulders, or it wouldn't fit on the back of his jersey. *(Perhaps that is why he got into lifting weights in the first place!)*

A PERSIAN POEM

At an event in Seattle, I wanted to add something new to my set. I quickly jotted down a very silly poem and delivered it to the crowd.

They laughed, and to my surprise, many asked if this

was printed anywhere they could purchase and share with their family.

It wasn't. But like a good entrepreneur, I have now fixed that. Behold. Here is that work of art just for you.

Move over Hafez. Buzz off Rumi. There's a new Persian poet in town...

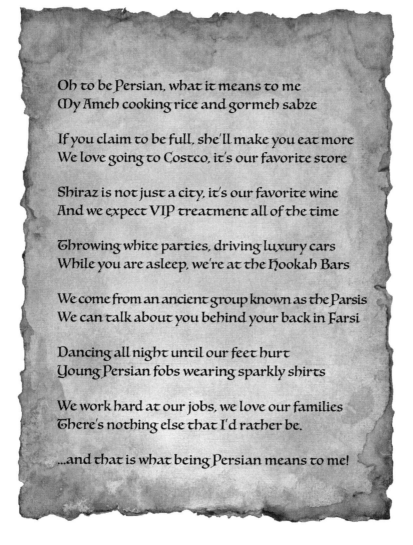

Oh to be Persian, what it means to me
My Ameh cooking rice and gormeh sabze

If you claim to be full, she'll make you eat more
We love going to Costco, it's our favorite store

Shiraz is not just a city, it's our favorite wine
And we expect VIP treatment all of the time

Throwing white parties, driving luxury cars
While you are asleep, we're at the Hookah Bars

We come from an ancient group known as the Parsis
We can talk about you behind your back in Farsi

Dancing all night until our feet hurt
Young Persian fobs wearing sparkly shirts

We work hard at our jobs, we love our families
There's nothing else that I'd rather be.

...and that is what being Persian means to me!

LAUGH 'TIL YOU CRY

Ask an Iranian to shed a tear over some poetry and they're happy to do it. Try to make them laugh, and now you've got your work cut out for you. One could say that making an Iranian laugh is like pulling teeth, but you'd be wrong. We have a lot of dentists in our community, so pulling teeth is actually much easier!

Luckily, just about every household has that one funny aunt or uncle who's always cracking jokes. If you have more in your family, count that as a blessing! If you don't have any, that means it's now your job.

I want to challenge you to be that funny family member. Greet everyone that walks through your door with a big smile. Learn how to tell a favorite joke. Practice often. Then keep adding material to your arsenal. It may not be easy at first, but eventually the people will be gravitating to you for much needed comic relief. SO THERE IT IS... That's your homework. I'M ASKING FOR YOUR HELP to bring some much needed laughter into the world.

CLOSING

You made it to the end! As I write this, whole regions of the Middle East are in turmoil *(what else is new)*. Religious extremists are murdering innocent civilians around the globe. Crazies of all cultural backgrounds continue to do despicable things. Worse yet, *people are "unfriending" each other over politics on FACEBOOK!* Meanwhile, the media are happily fanning the flames in the hopes of increased ratings.

The only way we win is if we come together, fight against their rhetoric, and believe it or not — *laugh.* Laughter is one of our biggest weapons. There is nothing strict regimes, extremists, and overly politically correct social justice warriors hate more than the sound of laughter. They've decided *(without our consent)* that humor is somehow immoral, impolite, or inappropriate and needs to be policed — but they are wrong.

With a well-crafted joke, *ANYTHING* can be funny. If discussed in a new, innovative, or creative way, PEOPLE WILL LAUGH. Now the radicals listed above have no choice but to throw a tantrum, pout, or reprimand you for your cheerful reactions. It kills them that despite their best efforts, they just can't control a genuine spontaneous outburst of joy.

In every James Bond movie, the villain has our hero bound, gagged, and ready for torture, but as soon as the duct tape is ripped from his mouth — *Bond starts laughing.* The ultimate confidence. He laughs because, no matter what they try, it simply isn't going to work. He knows a secret. He is about to turn the tables on them.

A sense of humor and a willingness to chuckle in the face of danger is just one of the many weapons we can use to fight against the forces that intend to drive us apart.

Let's not take the freedom to tell jokes and speak freely for granted. It is a powerful right we should cherish and use often. After all, there are people that don't have that opportunity who depend on us to keep it alive. We didn't earn this freedom, and we don't get to take it with us, so our job is to keep this torch alive for the short time it's in our care. Then dutifully pass it on to the next generation.

Here's to enough new laughs to fill another book, more fun times on stage, and many more positive multi-cultural memories to come. I'm comforted by the fact that no matter what is happening in the world, there will always be a comedian there, waiting...armed and ready — with a joke.

K-von is the most famous Half-Persian comedian (and now *writer*) in the world!

Millions have seen his appearances on NETFLIX with Russell Peters, NBC's Last Comic Standing, MTV, and his popular TEDx Talk. His style is versatile yet relatable with fun storytelling and high-energy performances about a variety of mainstream topics.

Check him out on **K-VONCOMEDY.COM**
or his popular **YOUTUBE.COM/KVONCOMEDY**

@KVONCOMEDY ON: 🐦 ▶️ f 📷 ✈️

We hope you enjoyed this book.
Be sure to check out K-von's other work:

"ONCE YOU GO PERSIAN..." AUDIOBOOK
Read by the Author with Bonus Features!

"TANX GOD!"
One-Hour Comedy Special

"NOWRUZ: LOST & FOUND"
Full Length Documentary

"WRISTS OUT"
One-Hour Comedy Special